Beaten Black and Blue

Born into Racism

AUGUSTE KNUCKLES

authorHOUSE®

AuthorHouse™ UK
1663 Liberty Drive
Bloomington, IN 47403 USA
www.authorhouse.co.uk
Phone: UK TFN: 0800 0148641 (Toll Free inside the UK)
        UK Local: 02036 956322 (+44 20 3695 6322 from outside the UK)

Published by AuthorHouse 09/17/2020

ISBN: 978-1-6655-8022-9 (sc)
ISBN: 978-1-6655-8023-6 (hc)
ISBN: 978-1-6655-8021-2 (e)

Print information available on the last page.

Any people depicted in stock imagery provided by Getty Images are models,
and such images are being used for illustrative purposes only.
Certain stock imagery © Getty Images.

This book is printed on acid-free paper.

Dedicated to my wife and our amazing children
I've been truly blessed.

CONTENTS

About the Author ix
The end of the beginning 1
Amuse Bouche 3
Sprouts 5
You're in the army now boy 10
Boot-Polish Black 11
Twenty-First Birthday Cocktail, Amsterdam. 15
Gold Fish 16
Abandoned 17
A fractured Mind 26
Cheesy Snacks 27
Popping Out for a Loaf of bread 30
Jerk Chicken Wings. 31
Two niggers 36
Soap Raped 37
Racists everywhere 41
Welcome to the World of cooking Part 1: A chef's introduction ... 42
The million-dollar question 47
Welcome to the World of cooking Part 2: The dancing CHEF 48
Dementia Plum Crumble 54
When Mental Health Said Hello 56
Miguel's Toys 61
Held at Gunpoint 66
Married to Cocaine, Part 1: The Love Affair Is Strong 70
Kissed by God 74

A chef losing the plot 76
Married to Cocaine, Part 2: It's how it all started, my love for
drugs. 79
Life in the Military: Ranks amongst Starch-Pressed Chefs............80
Chef's Equipment for War 87
The Frying Pan..90
Near-Death Experience 93
If it had been nerve gas, I would be dead 95
Prisoner of War...97
2007 101
Just Another Cocaine Session.. 107
Sweets... 109
The Rusty Bike... 110
It Really Did Happen 113
Ice cubes and Jack... 115
The Haziness of Reality..120
Waste of Time 124
Cocaine in a Nutshell...127
Sucker for Punishment 128
I Was Thinking About You..132
The Beginning 133
The journey hasn't ended 135

ABOUT THE AUTHOR

To have achieved the unachievable, to have finally spoken out and written these words, I sincerely hope my story gives victims, survivors of abuse and neglect courage. Regardless, don't let anyone tell you, you can't achieve great things no matter how big the obstacle. Auguste Knuckles 1st time author, who really doesn't consider himself an Author by the way.

THE END OF THE BEGINNING

January 2020, the day my world came crashing down around me. The cold dark blanket of suicide once again having its day, but this day he was all guns blazing. Thoughts so loud, thoughts so disturbing, telling me it would be over quickly; it would be quick, easy, and painless. *Nothing to worry about,* my thoughts were telling me. *Nothing to worry about.*

I'd never experienced anything as powerful or overwhelming as what was going on in my head, a full-blown, lightspeed, psychotic meltdown. *Just pull the car over onto the hard shoulder, exit the car, and walk head-on into rush hour traffic on the M25. Quick, easy, and painless. I promise you, this is as good as it gets. This is your time.*

Leaving behind a world I had struggled so hard to build, a world that was my wife and our beautiful children. My world that had given me so much love, something I seldom experienced as a child.

I thought my war had ended when I returned from the Middle East in 1991 having served as a soldier, a desert rat, during the first Gulf War. I was awarded a commendation by the commanding chief of the Allied Forces, the Gulf War medal and clasp, plus the liberation of Kuwait medal, all of which I sold to feed my addiction.

A dyslexic punching bag, a loner who had no place at school or at home, I found purpose through food. Classically trained, I went on to forge a career in the hospitality industry, working my way up the ladder to be executive head chef in some of the busiest and most prestigious hotels and restaurants in the United Kingdom.

After I had finally won the battle with drugs and alcohol, another

1

war had started, my war with mental health. It would have been easier to have put that bullet through my brain during the war. It's a war I'm still fighting to this day, diagnosed with complex post-traumatic stress disorder (CPTSD), anxiety, and obsessive-compulsive disorder (OCD) and all its side orders. I'm a fragile soul believe it or not, but I'm a survivor.

Writing this book hasn't been easy, but it has helped me put closure to some of my darkest flashbacks and nightmares. You see, I'm just the average guy on the street, trying to make his way through this complex enigmatic labyrinth called life. There was no way I was going to let my challenges stop me from telling my story. *Beaten Black and Blue* is the true story of my life.

AMUSE BOUCHE

When I sit and ponder my life as a boy, it brings tears to my eyes. What would I say if I could go back and speak with that scared, frightened little fella, if I could go back in time? "Run, hide, call the police, tell a family member, call a friend, tell a teacher." I was a child, I didn't know what to do. I find it hard to believe that no one saw the bruises, heard the cry for help, or saw the sadness behind my cheeky smile as a four-year-old boy. If the truth be told I believe they all saw what they decided to ignore, me.

I would say, "You will most certainly overcome the pain, but the biggest challenge will be dealing with the trauma as you grow through the decades into manhood and finally have children of your own."

It's been a turbulent journey, countless highs and lows, battling addiction, depression, anxiety, and my demons within. It has, in fact, been brutal suffering in silence, but I'm no longer frightened or unsure of what the future holds.

At the age of forty-something, I've finally found my voice. I've finally found a way to cope with the flashbacks, nightmares, and the mental, emotional, and physical abuse inflicted on me by the ones who should have protected me from harm. One could say I've found inner peace with the cold dark blanket of suicide, the last exit for so many lost souls.

I've finally willed the courage to speak. I've finally confessed to loved ones why I was disconnected, distant, fractured, and lost. It wasn't meant to be this way, I myself have hurt those closest to me, but others had a heavy hand that rained down on me. I'm not perfect, but if you smash a Ming vase and super glue it back together, its not going to be the same vase.

If I could go back and speak with those abusers and the ones who stood silently in the shadows and did nothing, what would I say? I wouldn't say anything. My life has been a rollercoaster of miracles, all of you who have lived in my shadow these past decades and witnessed the beauty which I have miraculously created and what I have experienced. It's all my abusers who have become silent, knowing that my presence in their lives is me tolerating every breath they take.

My journey of healing still requires ongoing therapy, medication, and assessments with various psychologists and doctors. My future has a new horizon, positive vibes, family and friends around me who love me and want to see me happy and healthy. If asked what has been achieved this past four decades, the cycle of hereditary abuse has finally been broken, and it was the unfortunate luck of a fragile four-year-old boy who did it.

This cooking malarkey has almost killed me, AK

SPROUTS

S prouts, what's the big deal with sprouts. As a chef during the festive season, having taste for a good sprout goes along way, especially when cooking for thousands of Christmas party guests. I would get my commis chefs to check that they were cooked and seasoned well before plating. A well-cooked sprout can either break or make a Christmas dinner. During my childhood, they would break me every single time Doris served them.

When I initially began to write this book, I remember every second, third, fifth word would either be "fuck", "cunt", "bastard", "wanker", or "twat". Swear words just poured out of me with such venom, coursing through my veins until finally released via my fingertips. I just held my head in my hands thinking, *why am I even thinking, let alone trying to complete such a project?* The fact I'm dyslexic made me very anxious. Thank god for spell check.

I suppose I wasn't mentally, emotionally, or physically ready to embark on such a journey. If the truth be told, I don't think I had truly processed the anger or the agony within. I don't think I will ever come to terms with my childhood, although I will have to process what has held me back all these years, addiction. All I pray and work for today is that I find some sort of peace within myself and be a true inspiration to my children.

My question to this day is, if you have a child who doesn't like a certain food item, why go to all the trouble persecuting them for hours on end at the dinner table in trying to force them to consume such an item?

I just didn't like sprouts, regardless of who cooked them or how they were cooked. I just had no love whatsoever for the humble baby cabbage. Over the decades of explaining the traumatic episode during my childhood to family and friends, the only comparison is the Russian roulette scene in one the most epic movies ever made, *The Deer Hunter.*

Sunday morning would start with our visit to church, Sunday school. I suppose it was the only chance for my parents to get a leg over living in such a small council house on the estate where we lived during the eighties. Five kids and two adults crammed into a three-bed semi-detached house like hundreds of other families living on the breadline.

One thing I did like about Sunday school was volunteering to go around and take up the collection. Main reason was I would skim at least a fiver from the collection to spend on sweets, custard creams, and crap during the school week. I'll go into that a bit later. Savage I know robbing from the church, I suppose that's why I like to give folding money as opposed to coins during Sunday mass today, my way of asking for forgiveness. Apologies you never got that new church roof.

Arrive home from church then off to the corner shop to buy cider and barley wine for Doris, and whatever else she needed to get through her day. I would make two or three journeys before and after dinner. Cider, I say. Yes, a ten-year-old off to buy alcohol for the grown-ups.

If the neighbours knew I was off to the shop, they would shout over the garden fence, "Oi treacle, can Deliveroo pick me up ten B&H and four cans of special brew?" Procuring fags and alcohol at the ripe old age of ten had been going on for a few years, so do the math, drink responsibly. Fuck that shit back in the eighties, all you shabby parents should have procured responsibly before considering a 24hr lock in.

So, she's in the kitchen, preparing and cooking dinner, smashed off her chops with a jaw at 9 o'clock. May I say for the record the kitchen on Sundays was out of bounds. If you did manage to get in, you would be met with a scolding slap with the wooden spoon that had sat in a pot of gravy for the best part of an hour.

Not only would you have a wooden spoon print across your chops for the remainder of the day, you would be scalped with the most horrific verbal abuse: "Get the fuck out the kitchen, you scroungy little bastard. Go on, fuck off. That's it, get the fuck out of the kitchen." Strange considering I didn't even get a foot in.

So, things are cooking up nicely before we go full wankered, full-on abuse is in the post for the kid who has no love whatsoever for baby cabbages. "Are we having sprouts?" I've spent many years trying to put into perspective what was going on in the household kitchen every Sunday. Lines of coke, a massive joint hanging out the kitchen window. Were there other people in there having a party? maybe I'll never know.

Five minutes before service there is a mad panic around the place, like a dysfunctional kitchen before service—mayhem, carnage, kids pull the table out, get it laid. Mad panic, me and my three siblings running around the gaff like headless waiters with two left feet. But who's got the balls to enter the kitchen to fetch the cutlery? The black sheep of the family has, though he's more like forced to enter the dreaded fortress. Shoved through the door by the ravaged hungry mod, gagging for lumpy mash.

I always used to think Doris was a decent chef, but looking back, I would be traumatised every other meal I was served. I remember sitting on a plastic chair, food thrown in front of us like we had to be grateful for what we were about to consume. Grateful. Grateful was beaten out of me every given chance. More like resentment for what I was forced to eat.

I don't ever remember meat being on my plate, was us kids' vegans? I always remember a juicy piece of meat being on Boris's plate. We've all witnessed a hungry dog attacking a bowl of dog meat; the dog goes bananas. Well imagine four starving kids going off over a plate of veg, mash, and lumpy gravy. My siblings would put a plate of food away in seconds while Boris lavished over his prime cut of whatever Doris happened to have purchased from the butchers.

Then the sprouts, food of the devil. This was when two bottles of cider and half a dozen cans of barley wine would kick in. I'd push the sprouts around my plate for the best part of thirty minutes. "Eat those fucking sprouts or else".

"I've worked my ass off for you stinking kids to put food on the fucking table," said Doris. As if I knew what a hard day's work was like. It was totally irrelevant how hard she had worked for a child to comprehend. Why would she be so fixated in trying to force-feed me something I couldn't stomach?

Three siblings polished off their food, slurp, slurp. Bosh, job done. "Please, I don't like the taste of sprouts mom".

"You're an ungrateful little bastard. You will not leave this table until those sprouts are eaten." Another thirty minutes pass. Cold sprouts. Boris splayed out on the couch, pushing out z's as loud as a jet. Siblings out in the yard playing ball. Another thirty minutes pass. She's on me like a rat on a Big Mac. In my face, her eyes blazing with hatred. "You fucking eat them now."

Sitting at the table with a revolver at my temple, scared as a kid riding the Pepsi max. A sick, twisted Doris in my face, sweating like a dyslexic on countdown, eyeballs glazed over. "Eat those fucking sprouts!" Palm of her hand smashes on the table. She must be warming up. I'd long gone pissed myself. Sodden, I'm frozen, crouching over a plate of cold sprouts, unable to speak let alone breathe.

I start to hyperventilate; an asthma attack is clearly on its way. Stressed beyond measure, whimpering, "I don't like sprouts," has no effect, I'm now full blown in her vortex.

The mad, crazed Vietnamese soldier is going off "Doris". A week in the bamboo cage submerged in a rat-infested waterway is looking inviting. I need to get off this table, out of this nightmare. Before I know it, she screams, "Right, fuck off to bed." One nil to Doris. Playtime is long gone, siblings back indoors. It's in the bath, one boiled kettle between four of us.

I remove myself from the empty table the size of a football pitch. Doris is slurping the last dregs from her cider bottle, mangled on the sofa. I haven't the energy to strip naked and climb into a bath of cold mud. I climb to the top bunk exhausted, shamed, lost. I cry myself to sleep knowing next Sunday will be the same barbaric insanity.

"Daddy."

"Yes, son?"

"I don't like sprouts."

"It's okay. I haven't put any on your plate."

"Thank you, Daddy. I love you."

YOU'RE IN THE ARMY NOW BOY

Fuck me what do we have here? A gollywog, the only gollywog in this squadron. From now on during training you are going to be known as jigaboo, do you here me boy? Yes sergeant, he's no place on this parade square, he marches like a monkey.

BOOT-POLISH BLACK

During long hot summers back in the eighties, I couldn't sleep at night due to my asthma, It was difficult at times. Doris always insisted I go to bed with my younger siblings. My elder sister would be out and about, hanging out with other teenagers her age, black, white, mixed-race, Asian, and ethnic kids. Black like me, brown just like me.

As soon as my siblings fell asleep, I would sneak out of bed, crawl along the landing, hide or be as invisible as possible, and watch TV from the top of the stairs. Haven't a clue what I'd be watching, thinking about it, most likely racist comedians, telling jokes about anyone who wasn't like them, but I would sit there. Any decent mother would have known I was at the top of the stairs and most likely would have invited me down—if I was on my best behaviour and I didn't make a sound.

I heard Boris and Doris talking in the living room, the thought today makes me sick. The pair of them plotting their assault on my sister when she returned home. The estate was multicultural, and my sister hung out with likeminded teenagers like herself, we didn't no racism, we were born into it. You only know it's meaning when you are old enough to understand the magnitude of the word.

Just for the record, Boris and Doris were white. My two younger siblings, half siblings, were white. My older sister was white, I was black, "half-breed", "mixed-race", "crusty". Although I hadn't a clue what my heritage was, so I can't go there at this stage.

There was a knock at the door. I was still watching whatever I was watching from the top of the stairs. I hear him ask Doris, "Are you ready?" Most likely he's given her a wink and a nod for confirmation that she's okay with the barbarian punishment about to be laid down.

My sister hadn't even stepped foot in the house when she was grabbed by the scruff of her neck and dragged through the door two feet off the ground. For the record, I need to mention this bully of a man, Boris, isn't even her father. The woman sat on her drunken, twisted, sick, and toxic ass is her biological mother.

I didn't get it then, and I will never understand how or why Doris would allow her child to be beaten up by a man who was not even the father. What kind of woman would you have to be to allow this to happen. It was carnage—pure, unadulterated carnage—and I sat at the top of the stairs, witnessing this in my own home.

Decades later, Doris would cower behind a large glass of whisky or wine and blame him. Yes, she blamed Boris. No, she let this happen, and to this day, I'm convinced she probably got some sort of twisted pleasure witnessing two of her children being battered. If not, why didn't she put herself between him and me and my elder sister. Why didn't she say, "No! Don't you fucking dare touch my kids"?

My sister was dragged into the kitchen, screaming, "Let me go." I was frozen, still invisible at the top of the stairs. I can hear my sister's screams to this day, Doris did nothing. She just sat on her ass, on her sofa.

He grabbed the black shoe polish from beneath the sink. My sister screamed, "No! Leave me alone. Don't do it. Please, please, Mom help me!" Once he got hold of the polish, my sister would be dragged into the living room, still screaming. Then he would rub black boot polish into her face.

I couldn't do anything, I was scared, totally and utterly frozen. Should I have gone downstairs and pleaded with him to stop, no, because guaranteed he would lay into me. After all, he had laid into me for less when I was a child.

"You want to hang out with those black fucking losers, darkies" he would shout, "maybe we should paint you fucking black, so you can be like them." A wooden spoon would be broken over her back.

Boot polish all over my sister's face, tears—so many tears—and cries for help, but she just sat there.

I'd run back to my bunk and try and hide under the bedsheets scared, so scared, that he would continue his rage and come upstairs. I lost count how many times this happened over the years. It was surreal, but this was going on; it was going on. I started to have issues with the colour of my skin. I was having issues with my identity, issues with me being me. I began to hate myself for being black because I saw what my sister was subjected to because of boys like me. It was the ultimate head fuck for a child to witness. I felt worthless, I wanted to die.

Having children of my own with the most amazing wife, I just can't and will never understand why a parent would want to beat down on their children. I know it happens, and it's fucking wrong on all levels. Knowing full well they will be left with emotional, mental, and physical scars for the remainder of their lives. Or was it just an eighties thing. No, it wasn't just an eighties thing. This was the result of generational abuse, on a level engraved so deep. Her life had taken on a direction that I believe she still regrets to this day, when she lay with my biological father. Regret, she sought closure by allowing the abuse of her children by a sick and twisted individual, as if I was the one to blame for her shenanigans.

Now I'm not going to say I was an angel by any means. I was dealing with serious issues, so when I was given advice to seek help, I went and got help, took me a few years, but I got help. You can lead a donkey to water, but whether he decides to drink that water is down to the donkey. I drank the water. Not the donkey's water, but you know where I'm coming from.

Doris had the audacity to sit there crying, usually at family get-togethers with the biggest audiences. Obviously drunk, she would make out she was the victim. "I couldn't do anything", she would mumble from behind her glass, expecting all of us to feel sorry for her. She *didn't* do anything. Doris could have prevented the beatings and abuse. She knows full well that lying blatantly through her teeth doesn't cut it anymore, not with me anyways.

It's a bit late in life, after you've been to hell and back and then gone back for more, to want to be subjected to more lies on the other end of a phone call, listening to someone wanting to tell you she's sorry. Sorry, really? This boy is already baked. You can't go back adjust a few ingredients and pop him back in the oven, no, not unless your Marty Mcfucking Fly

I see hundreds of thousands of people protesting that black lives matter in the world today. Racism shouldn't exist, but it does. As a dual-heritage man, I can't help but go back to the top of those stairs in that toxic putrid house, on that god-forsaken estate we were dragged up and not think about my life. I was born into racism and have witnessed it first-hand within the family who raised me, so how could I not be affected, affected is an understatement, so yes, if asked, do black lives matter, hell yeah. #BLM

TWENTY-FIRST BIRTHDAY COCKTAIL, AMSTERDAM.

Ingredients

1 gram of PCP
2 grams cocaine
6 Love doves
4 LSD tads banana splits
2 grams speed
1 bottle Jack Daniels
8 tumblers
1 ounce of purple haze for the journey
1 Defibrillator

Method

Take all ingredients except Jack Daniels, purple haze and defibrillator, crush in a pestle and mortar. When all ingredients are combined, divide between tumblers. Fill the glasses with Jack Daniels and consume. I would strongly suggest you do not try this dish unless you are accompanied by an adult.

GOLD FISH

At the depths of addiction, there is no line to cross, there are no boundaries, there is no filter, no man's land is all around you. The world inside your goldfish bowl, with a broken windscreen wiper screeching as it rubs across the glass bowl on the outside is the only thing that makes sense, that and doing more cocaine. The world around you is plugged into a moon sized speaker, jacked up, the quiver travels through you at lightning speed, unable to string a sentence together, you stand silent, drinking yourself into a coma. **AK**

ABANDONED

'm a chef by trade, I've been cooking professionally since the age of seventeen. That's when I started my first proper paid job within Her Majesty's Forces, Army Catering Corp (ACC). The ACC no longer exists; the army bought in contractors. It's a shame. Although we were called 'slop jockeys', we cooked some seriously good-quality food for the boys.

Considering there was never much about the household when we were kids, and that number two always had different food than us kids at mealtimes, food seemed so appealing to me, "why wouldn't it black Olive Twist". The love for food came about during my home economics classes at school. I would rock up to class with a bag of whatever I could scrounge from around the house or shoplift from the local corner shop. At the end of class, I would have made either spring rolls, some sort of Chinese stir fry, a gateau or sponge cake decorated with buttercream, fresh fruit, and chocolate garnishes.

Long story short, my home economics teacher spoke with Doris during the school holidays. Then boom, I was enrolled at the catering community college across town. I enrolled in 1985 and studied classical French cuisine, patisserie, and food and beverage service for the hospitality industry.

General Certificate of Secondary Education (GCSE)
English—ungraded
History—ungraded
Maths—ungraded

Rural Science—ungraded
Craft Design Technology—ungraded
Home Economics Theory—ungraded, practical (pass)

If you subject a child to extreme levels of mental, physical, and emotional abuse, there will be some serious issues with school. This showed in my school grades and when I did finally leave school. In the words of so many teachers and my dysfunctional family, I was going to be a loser, a nobody, a dead beat.

It makes me laugh today. My uncle Henry, as flash as he was back then with the sports cars, the cool designer clothes his lavish lifestyle, was the only one laughing and joking about me being beaten black and blue, when he visited us. Where is Henry today? On the fucking bread line, picking litter off the street.

I had zero confidence throughout my teens, no self-esteem, no willpower to do anything. If it wasn't for my home economics teacher, Mrs Buxton, bless her soul, I would have most likely drifted in and out of trouble and juvenile centres. I most likely would have ended up in a young offender's centre, last stop prison, most likely spending many years as someone's wife and then on to an early grave.

Thinking about it, back then Doris never encouraged me to do anything, nothing, and I mean fuck all. She might have dragged me uptown a few times to carry shopping bags and forced me to join the army cadets, but apart from that, there wasn't much going on.

As a chef I've worked in some amazing restaurants with Michelin-star chefs, stunning hotels across the globe, and cruise ships. I have been fortunate to have travelled extensively. I also ran my own restaurant in Spain for two years with two business partners I met working as a private chef in the Alps circa 2000.

In 2016 I was working at a beautiful hotel in Marlow as a pastry chef, something different than my usual line of employment as an executive head chef. I think I just needed a change to get me out the office and away from doing all the mundane jobs we executive head chefs hate but had to do. Budgets, forecasting, meetings, strategizing, Human resources, development and meetings about meetings, plus getting extremely smashed at staff parties. I needed to get back to some form of cooking, get back to my love for food.

Working through an agency, the pay wasn't bad, but nothing like I'd earned before. How I saw it was if the bills were covered, there was food on the table, and I had change for petrol, I was happy taking orders from someone else for a change. Not having much responsibility, able to create beautiful desserts, afternoon teas, and assist with weddings and functions across the estate was a winner.

I had been at the hotel for several months, and our second child, was cooking nicely in the wife's belly oven. I can't remember the exact date, but I received a phone call from a prestigious agency for chefs regarding a vacant position in a beautiful, four-star, deluxe hotel in the West Midlands.

My résumé was online on various social media platforms. You must keep yourself out there as you never know which general manager is looking for a well-seasoned, experienced, down-to-earth, open-minded, hands-on chef to revitalize their culinary department.

Several phone calls and three interviews later, plus several discussions with my wife about working away from home for a few years, I was finally appointed the new executive head chef for the beautiful property. I started employment in the third quarter of 2016.

I travelled up the M40 from Berkshire to Birmingham first thing Monday morning and did what chefs do—meetings, strategizing, menu development, forecasting and budgeting, scheduling, speaking with clients and suppliers, and the odd bit of cooking. I then travelled back down the M40 Friday afternoons. Sometimes I cruised down the M1 to mix up the scenery a little. The M40 can be a drag; it's as flat as Belgium.

The one condition I was hesitant about in taking this new position on was having to move back in with Doris as the hotel was a short drive from her house, it was the only sensible option, otherwise I would have to rent an apartment near the hotel. So, to save a few grand I moved in during the week.

Moving back into my old bedroom was going to have its challenges. The main one was getting on with Doris again. Or maybe it would be a chance for her to explain herself as to why I was battered left, right, and centre, how wrong was I? I had more chance of making love to a merman.

The first few months flew by. Doris was now married to Alfred and a carer for her mother, the one and only evil Phillis, a former member of the SS death squad. By the way if there are any Nazi hunters out there this isn't true. Its just the anger within me trying to express what she did and how I feel about her. Phillis was in full-blown dementia. She wore a nappy at night and during the day, dressed in her designer clothes, sat propped up in her chair in the naughty corner. There she sat day in day out, month after month, year after year. Phillis often called me her son. Or she would ask, "Look at the handsome young man. Who is he? What's he doing here? Is it Christmas?" Dribble, dribble, more dribble. She thought I was her father at one stage and a past lover. Although dementia was having its day, Phillis knew everything going on under her nose.

Doris and Alfred loved a drink, and I mean "a drink." They were often on the pop from the crack of dawn until they crashed in the afternoon. Often when I arrived home after an early shift, it wasn't surprising if they were all tucked up by 5 p.m. with a leftover takeaway of some sort in the dog bowl.

What I witnessed during my time back at that house absolutely set in concrete how angry and sometimes evil Doris was. I often arrived home after work tired and needed to rest. But she would be going off, going off the fucking rails, lost the fucking plot, mental going off. Doris screamed abuse at Alfred. "Get away from me you fucking cunt".

On and on and on, who the fuck are you? You fucking disgust me, you fucking horrible bastard." She would also lose it with Phillis, and I mean physically and mentally abuse the old lady. Regardless, it's not on. Doris would of course, also lose it with me, screaming up the stairs to my room, "You're no fucking good either, you fucking bastard, who the fuck do you think you are, you can fuck off out of here, ya bastard". Sheer hatred and anger pouring out from her mouth, it was savage at times, some nights I Just left and slept in the hotel, leaving her to continue her onslaught.

It's ironic after what Phillis did all those decades back that she forced her grown daughter to give me up, yet I was there, standing between them both, shouting at Mother to calm the fuck down and back off, or I'd call the police and social services if the abuse didn't stop. Phillis in a care home, a *One Flew over the Cuckoo's Nest*-type place, and Doris banged up in solitary for being a nutter, a lunatic.

Now what I'm about to say hasn't been dressed up like a beautiful line-caught salmon, poached, garnished, and ready for a million-dollar banquet. It's the truth. Just for the record, I had no intention back then, when shacked up with Murdock in writing a book. My only intention was to do well within my employment and embrace my wife and kids when I arrived home Friday afternoons.

Every other week and obviously smashed on grapes, during conversation Doris would mumble, "They made me do it. They fucking made me do it, fucking bastards."

"Made you do what? What the fuck did they make you do? Who made you do what?" I would ask.

"Tell him, tell him the truth," Alfred would say. But she never did. This bullshit went on for months, until one evening I sat with her and asked her face-to-face, "What the fuck did they make you do?"

"What the fuck are you going on about. Made you do what?" Then out it came.

"When you were born, I had to take you to my parents' house because I had nowhere to go after I knifed him in the face with a kitchen knife."

"What the fuck? Knifed your then husband in the face? Fuck me. Talk about a psycho."

"We just had to go there, you, me, and your sister. But my parents, your grandparents, persecuted me every day about having a black baby in the house. They couldn't stand having you there. You were a shame on the family,"

This was just bonkers but considering the climate in the United Kingdom in the early seventies, mixed-marriages and half-breed kids in some circles were not good for morale. Not good at all. I had been born into a family of Enoch Powell supporters, BNP, you name it. It wouldn't surprise me if Phillis had a picture of the man himself hanging in the kitchen, Enoch or Adolf.

How can a baby be a shame on the family? I mean seriously. This went on for months and months. "They fucking hated you being in there house, so they gave me an ultimatum," Doris told me. "Can you fucking believe this? Well this isn't Hollywood, people. This isn't *Different Strokes*. We both leave, or you leave."

"Leave me? Leave me where? Where would I leave to? Where would a baby go? Nightclubbing? It's not like I could make a few sandwiches, wrap them in a handkerchief, and head on out the door like Huckleberry Finn on one of his merry adventures through KKK country."

My blood started to boil. My pulse became erratic, and beads of sweat poured from my brow because the bitch who orchestrated this—Phillis—sat in the next room. The woman I had defended from her own daughter not even a month ago, the fucking SS commander and racist bitch, sat dribbling in the next room, thinking I was her ex-lover.

"So, what did you do."

"I abandoned you."

"What do you mean, you abandoned me? What, like wrapped me in a blanket and left me outside a charity shop with a sign around my neck, 'Please help me'?"

"Your grandparents."

"Stop. No, no, stop there. They couldn't be my grandparents. They're savages."

"They just couldn't bear the thought of sharing their household with a baby like you". We drove to Johnny's barracks. He was waiting at the gates, and I just handed you to him and walked away." I'm fucking gobsmacked. "I handed you, my baby, to him like a packed fucking lunch. You were screaming, screaming so loud Auguste everyone was watching. You were trying to cling to me. It was horrible; you wouldn't let me go."

"I didn't have anyone but you, my fucking mother, that cold dark winters day you threw me to the wolves! I was your baby; your flesh and blood and you threw me, your baby to the wolves. And boy did they feast on me."

Now for the record, I've seen the sunny snaps with them both in nice locations. I was sitting on laps, all smiley, happy. So, what? who gives a fuck, I really don't care. I've seen pictures of Adolf Hitler with Eva Braun holidaying in the Austrian alps, but that doesn't change anything, does it now? He was still a first-class genocidal maniac. So those coastal glamping pictures, go fuck.

For the record this wasn't your typical abandonment, drop him off with this selfish, irresponsible fella. No. From what I've been told, he then took me to his current wife's house, whom he already had kids with. I believe it was somewhere in Scotland. He dropped me off like a dirty pair of knickers. I'm not her son; I'm the bastard he's just had with another woman behind her back. Why on earth would she want a bastard about the house? and she didn't, the abuse begins.

I was abandoned for years. Out there, Imagine that. Imagine being told that as a man with children of my own. The trauma alone as a baby is too much to bare. I've watched my son for hours, days, playing with his toys, being cheeky, and getting up to mischief, the lovable bundle of joy he is to us both and his big sister. It just doesn't compute that I could abandoned him, let alone our daughter. Wrap them up like a fish supper with a side order of mushy peas with pickled onions and leave them outside the YMCA. It just doesn't register anywhere.

I soon resigned my post in Birmingham. It didn't end well due to my mental state. I still regret how it ended, as some of my work colleagues were spot on. but my head was mangled. I couldn't bear to be within spitting distance of Doris, let alone that toxic, demented cunt of a woman—Phillis—who wanted me banished.

Fast-forward to 2020 a new decade. The previous three years were dreadful. Adíos; thank God that's over. Little did we know we would be slapped sideways with COVID-19. I mean, did God see that coming? Maybe. Did the chefs cooking up bat soup, pangolin stir fry with a side of crispy cats' ears and sweet and sour monkey chops? They should have. Wrong on all levels or is there something more sinister behind the pandemic? I mean what's more sinister than raping and burning the place we call home.

After the most horrific, lightning-speed psychotic meltdown driving home from work January 2020—and minutes away from ending my life on the M25 during rush hour—it was time for me to get some serious help. I needed serious help. I needed Gandalf the Grey and White. I needed Obi-wan Kenobi. I would have settled for Nurse Ratchet.

Over the course of treatment, I spoke with my elder sister and asked if we could talk about what she witnessed and if she knew about the abuse inflicted on me as a baby. So, we spoke. It crippled me, but I had to hear it, I needed to know if its was real, or all made up in my mangled head.

We spoke openly for about thirty minutes about general COVID-19 stuff before I dived in. She asked, "Are you sure you want to hear this?" Yes, I'm sure, I needed to know, I began. I do know I was abandoned for some time. During this time, Doris had moved up north from down south somewhere after divorcing Bob, the guy who thought I was his child when I popped out. Then she linked up with Boris. White dude, white woman Doris, back to Bobs surprise, maternity ward, out pops the wrong colour baby with an afro. They divorce because he can't bear the fact his wife has done the dirty and slept with a chap that had no place at Phillis's house. Yes, a darkie.

"I'm abandoned; we've done that part. But now I'm about to be bought back to Doris because I'm being seriously abused. Physically, verbally, emotionally battered. Now when I say, "seriously abused", I mean seriously abused. I'm finally reconnected with her and my sister—you—and the man who is going to make the next ten years of my life agonisingly painful, Boris. I'm rushed into the car. Doris is frantic, shouting to her new man, 'Get us out of here!' Sister is on the back seat, bonkers, screaming. Boris is also having a meltdown. I'm sure he's thinking, *What the fuck am I getting into? I've just hooked up with this broad, and I've inherited two fucking sprogs, one of them a halfbreed."*

Mother tore my jump suite off in a panic. I couldn't possibly imagine what my sister was going through, but she said I was covered in bruises and bite marks, battered, not in good shape, not in good shape at all. Looking at photos taken around that time, I would say I was no older than three. There are only two reasons I've surmised why I was in such a state. One, I was mauled by dog, due to my fear of dogs as a young boy. Or two, I was mauled by a human. Who, why, what, where, and when have never been explained to me. A baby passed from home to home, with no medical records or fixed abode, out there, for the sick pleasure of others.

A FRACTURED MIND

Soon as we enter the playground our little ones are off playing happily with the other children in the park. Two dark figures come in to focus wielding machetes. Before I could even move, one figure has mutilated several small children. The playground is a war zone, baby arms and legs strewn everywhere. A young mother has been decapitated by the other figure who then focuses on my little boy. Screams echo through my body, paralyzed, I can't do anything to prevent the carnage. "babe, babe, come on we have to leave the kids are hungry". I'm snapped out of another walking nightmare. Ok babe, I'm coming.

CHEESY SNACKS

Amsterdam to Germany, Germany to Amsterdam, early nighties. Before the big raid on military barracks across Germany after the Gulf War, to try and catch naughty soldiers like myself and band of druggie square heads, smuggling copious amounts of drugs into Germany as a squaddie was as easy as putting on a pair of drill boots.

I lost count of the trips I made to Amsterdam during my four-year posting, but it was a lot. The crazy thing is I didn't even have a driving licence. Imagine that, driving around Europe with no licence. Mental, proper mental. Talk about my head being somewhere else. But my military pass sufficed.

One evening me and a few chums made a last-minute dash for the 'Dam. The club named chocolate was the place to be; everything and anything was the norm there. I had been to a dozen gay clubs in Germany during the early nineties. Hardcore Frankie Goes to Hollywood with a dash of Priscilla, Queen of the Desert. All the gay clubs had the best DJs, music, and yes, the best drugs.

Itinerary: arrive Amsterdam, get smashed, procure drugs, get more smashed, go clubbing, get more smashed. Sleep in the car or smoke weed until we pass the fuck out. Wake up, public toilet, freshen up, breakfast, smoke weed, procure weed, solid and chemicals, coke, e's, PCP, speed and acid, and whatever else the goody-goody man is selling, pair of fake Ray Bons, maybe a beach towel. Don't mind if I do.

Smoke weed, begin the journey back to Germany. I've realised I'm carrying a load of olives and pickles—drugs—a lot more than I normally did. Panic doesn't set in as I'm peeled as a banana, up in smoke, dusted. Pit stop a few clicks from the border—toilet break, super-large coffee, mouthwash, munchies.

I purchase a family-size pack of cheesy puffs, a huge fucking bag, munchies, almost at the border we start to get restless, a tad, pockets full of delicious treats. The nutter on the back seat has a panic attack. "What if we get pulled over, and we get searched. I'm smashed, man, I'm really fucking smashed." Help me fella's, someone fucking help me.

"That will never happen, dude. We are squaddies." Universal soldiers, Jean Claude Van fucking Dam bollocks man.

"Fuck that, dude. There's no way I'm doing six months in a military prison, getting spit roasted by two hairy engineers. It just isn't going to happen." I'm a virgin man.

"What isn't going to happen, the get nicked part or you having your back doors smashed in by a hairy engineer?

Okay, fuck it. Let's take no chances. So, I empty the all the cheesy puffs into my foot well. "Right, boys. Pass me all your stash. Hide what you can down your pants." I fill the empty bag with our side orders and top it off with cheesy puffs. I sling the rest out the window. Bosh, we are at the border.

Casual as a dog pissing on a lamp post, we pull the car up to immigration and show our military passes. Now, seen from a short distance, what I have in my hands is a bag of what appears to be cheesy puffs. And that's what I have, cheesy puffs. "gutten morgan mine frund, where are you traveling from?"

"Football game in Hengelo. Good game. Not too schabby." I offer the immigration officer my snacks. "Would you care for a cheesy puff?"

"Nine danka, I've just eaten mine frushstuck." Passes handed back to us, a nod, and we are free to go about our business. As we leave Amsterdam behind, to celebrate our juvenile ways, we all pop two tabs of acid, crank up the tunes and rave our way back to base.

Years later, after leaving the military, we all met at a rugby match in Twickenham. There was more cocaine being consumed that day than I've ever experienced. It was colossal. Walking around Tesco's, buying booze for the game, we did lines on top of display freezers. It was nuts, it was fucking pathetic. We spoke about the time we all dropped the two acid tabs. Looking back, we were never the same fellas after that trip to the 'Dam. Acid that strong, bonkers, proper bonkers, twitchy, twitchy eye syndrome.

Those who dance are considered mad by those who cannot hear the music, we were dancing and getting away with murder, I don't think anyone heard our tune.

POPPING OUT FOR A LOAF OF BREAD

When someone has a full blow addiction, it takes over. Procuring more drugs can be the main reason for getting out of bed in the afternoon. Much of the day is spent trying to think of ways to get more. I would do anything, absolutely anything to get out of the house to buy cocaine. I would pour all the milk down the sink, flush the bread down the toilet, make up all sort of bullshit to have an excuse. "Babe, I must go back to work, fire alarm has gone off, be back in thirty minutes." It would take at least an hour round trip to purchase the Bolivian, but fuck it, I needed it. I had to have it at all costs.

Friday night was a loaf of bread night once the little one went down. Out the door, brown or white babe and on my journey across town, I would literally be hyperventilating. My palms sweating, my balls tingling, and butterflies danced in my stomach (or maybe they were doing the pole vault). I was gagging for my fix.

When I finally arrived home, I didn't care about how many calls from my wife I had missed, let alone how to explain why I didn't have the loaf of bread I supposedly went out to buy. I got my fix and that's all I cared about. Cocaine was the love of my life, I didn't care if she cheated on me with millions of others, she gave me what I needed.

JERK CHICKEN WINGS

As far as irresponsible parents can push the boundaries of being irresponsible, sending your two children alone to parts of the United Kingdom on coaches to spend time with one's auntie and uncle, or in my sister's case, with her dad, is the premier league of irresponsibleness.

Before I continue, marching your children—eight and six years old—to the coach station and throwing them on a coach with a sandwich and a pound to Victoria Station from middle England is mad. When we arrived at Victoria, pockets full of random shit we stole from the service station, my sister would put me on my coach then head off to Cornwall. It doesn't happen today. It just doesn't happen. Back then it did, without a care in the world, off we went, so Boris and Doris could spend time together alone and with their new-born sons without two bastards about the house. I've thought about this endlessly over the years. Did they care for us? Well you're this far in the book, so you can guess the answer.

These shenanigans went on for years. Every half term from school and any other possible break, I'd be off. Bags packed, dumped on a coach, and sent to Ipswich. With regards to my sister, as mentioned, she was sent away to spend time with her biological father. Me? I was sent away for one specific reason, and that reason being I was an embarrassment and that bastard Boris didn't want me snivelling around the house all summer.

I'm no psychologist, and I don't have any experience whatsoever in psychology except for what I've experienced in being treated by psychologists and various doctors. But I believe this being sent away whenever possible, and everything else I was being subjected to, had a serious impact on me. I am, in fact, the manifestation of their neglect. So, what the fuck happened, what was happening around or above us. Was there some greater power at work here? Me and my sister could have easily been plucked from that coach by a paedophile, gagged in a dark cellar and ganged rape for weeks or until we bleed out.

A ticking time bomb started during my first unmanned mission to Ipswich at that tender age of 7. I began to lose all sense of who or what I was, where I was going, and why I was always being sent away. Basically, Doris wanted me out of her pathetic existence. But where did I belong? There was no father figure, no role model to look up to. There was no one I could call "Dad," Pops," "Father." There was only and always will be my auntie Stella. Regardless of how hardcore she was in her youth, she treated me like her own.

Doris never mentioned anything about my biological father, Johnny, until I was eleven, maybe twelve. What I remember from her failed attempt to explain I wasn't Boris's child went down like the titanic.

I really didn't give a fuck. I really didn't care what she was trying to say. I was beyond caring. I was a child who had been systematically broken-down month after month, year after year, by her and everyone who was a cunt. I was a victim of child abuse, relentless, non-stop abuse on all levels, Doris could have said my father was Father Christmas; it would not have made any difference.

Before I continue, I want to apologise to anyone reading this. If I could be more eloquent in explaining myself throughout this book, this project, I would. But I'm no Hunter S. Thompson or Bret Easton Ellis. I'm just me, trying to tell my story to the best of my ability. So please excuse me if this comes across as if it's been written by a dyslexic twelve-year-old who just turned forty.

Yes, where was I? Seemed to have gone around the houses there for a minute. That's it. I'm was starting to contemplate who I was, where was I from, Africa the Caribbean, any country where black people came from. I didn't know my heritage. I didn't have a clue, and

Doris didn't want to tell me. Doris didn't even know where he was from; no one did, only he did, and she didn't even know his proper name. So, I started thinking that I could have been adopted. I would have taken that on the chin any day. Maybe Doris adopted me, why wasn't anyone telling anything, or did I belong to someone else, knowing what I know now, it would not be a surprise me.

When I turned twenty-four, I met Johnny for the first time, totally random. No rush there then. The first question I asked was where the fuck he had been and where the fuck he was from. "I'm from Jamaica, son." Happy days, a rubber stamp on my forehead. "I'm from Jamaica." Finally, after spending two decades thinking I was from Barbados, I now have some form of Identity. I had just won countdown.

Where I belonged was a simple fact in my head—with my auntie Stella and her family. She was white. Her vivacious, charismatic, outgoing, handsome husband was black, and both their children— my cousins, my beautiful cousins—were the same colour as me, mixed race, dual heritage, half cast, toffee-caramel-brown. I fitted beautifully into the mix, so why wouldn't I call this home?

I had some sort of belonging. I truly felt part of the family; I *was* part of the family, and that Middle England only existed in my worst nightmares. But I'm fully aware it was not a nightmare; it was reality. From as young as I can remember, we did family things together with auntie Stella, my first life experiences. Good, healthy experiences happened in Ipswich. Everything was meaningful. I felt part of something. I felt free to be me without repercussions, or a slap for laughing out loud.

I can remember like it was yesterday spending long hot summers with my auntie Stella. She bought me and my cousins easy riders which provided access on all public transports across town. We travelled all over, visiting sports centres, parks, museums, outdoor swimming pools. Out all day, meeting friends and doing all the great stuff kids love to do. I had friends, not like the wankers I hung out with on that dreadful estate. Well maybe a few were okay, but the rest were wankers.

During the evenings, we hung out with other kids on the street, playing games, listening to music—Lose Ends was my favourite band during the eighties—and just generally had a good time. Returning home to Middle England a few days before school opened after the summer holidays was awful. I fucking hated it. Back to having my soul destroyed. The black kid within a family that within itself was, beyond doubt, proper fucked.

So here we go, and here it begins. In the most sarcastic of half-drunk voices, Doris asked, "What have you been up to all summer? Fuck all, I bet." Like she really cared. I mean really cared what I had been up to. It was her chance, her opportunity to ridicule me, embarrass me in front of everyone, and I mean everyone. And she loved it. Even my snivelling little half-siblings joined in.

Even if Phillis was or wasn't there, or if the neighbours happened to pop round for a drink, it was her sick and twisted sense of power over me. Toxic then and still toxic now. She even embarrassed me at my wedding. My wedding was her opportunity to spend time with her eldest daughter as opposed to spending time with me, my new wife, and her grandkids.

"Wedding day." "If it's okay, Auguste, I would like to sit and spend time with your sister as I don't see her often." Over the past 20 years Doris, has visited me twice, the second time being my wedding. My in-laws gave us £3,000 as a wedding gift. Doris, Alfred, and Phillis gave us £30. I didn't even bother to read the card because I know one of my half-siblings received twenty times that for his 3rd wedding, yes 3rd wedding gift. We would have settled for a bathmat.

I remember my auntie Stella and the gang enjoying jerk-style chicken wings for lunch one summer. I had never tasted anything like that before. Well what black kid would have tasted or heard of jerk spice growing up with the mashed potato and lumpy gravy soggy sprout family?

This was something new, something different. So, I told Doris, "5, 4, 3, 2, 1, lift off fucking chicken wings." It was like I had told the world's best joke. She laughed and laughed. "Chicken fucking wings. Have you fucking heard this you lot?" She was hysterical.

Every second word was, "fucking," and ended with, "chicken wings," or, "chicken wings fucking".

Imagine Oliver Twist receiving a beautiful roast chicken dinner, with all the trimmings, more trimmings than a Harvester salad bar. Could you imagine the look on his face? Could you imagine the smile he would have? Maybe his smile would be too big for his face. Well that was those chicken wings for me, and she fucking killed it.

SOAP RAPED

My wife loves a bath. Me personally, unless I'm in a Turkish sauna eating baklava then it's showers all day long. Something in me just doesn't register when it comes to having a bath. Not even a well-deserved soak after a shift on the pans followed by service. Smelly candles, Barry White playing, bliss, no, not bliss, not for this kid.

I've mentioned already that everything was different for Boris. He got first-class treatment, he flew 1st class every day and we got what was left over, the scraps and on many occasions, his dirty bathwater to wash ourselves in before bed.

My auntie Stella hated Boris, absolutely hated him. She knew what was going on; she knew everything. My auntie always knew who my biological father was. I am baffled to this day that during all my summers in Ipswich, he was just down the road. Maybe it was him, maybe he didn't want nothing to do with me.

It was decided between Boris and Doris that I would have nothing to do with Johnny, my biological father. Boris would raise me as his own; that was the deal. I would be kept away from Johnny and wouldn't be told anything, not even his name, not his background, or where he was from.

Raise me as one of his own. Why would someone who painted my sister with black boot polish beat her with every kitchen utensil raise a half-breed as one of his own? I was kid growing up with no soul, no purpose, no direction, no ambitions, no one interested in my well-being apart from my auntie Stella, the phenomenal woman.

She could see the pain in my eyes, the hurt, but she couldn't do anything because Mother wanted it that way and forced my auntie not to say shit. My auntie could only give me the love, the same love she gave to her kids during my time with them. It was priceless. Its probably what kept me alive knowing the six-week school holidays we spent together and then the odd half-term break would recuperate me until I returned to no child's land.

Going way back, back to my first memories as a child, there is one memory that stands out, and its not a happy memory. Walking to school alone at the age of five or six was the norm. Well it was the norm for me because I don't remember any other kids walking alone.

Even at my pass-out parade from the army, I was the only soldier whose parents were absent. Totally embarrassed during the pass out reception, the only soldier making up excuses as why my, I'm going to hate saying this word "parents" where absent, and there I'm stood making up fucking excuses for them both. Good thing about the army, it gave me things I had never experienced before—belonging, three seriously good meals per day, structure, and the ability to believe in myself. The fights, the fascists, the racists wankers, the bumps and bruises, the scrapes I sustained during infantry training, my sergeant screaming down my ear every waking minute of the day wasn't anything I couldn't handle. Standard procedure for a kid dragged up on an estate called Pet Cemetery.

I remember walking home from school one grey cloudy day. It's mad because it always seemed grey in Middle England, always grey. I had soiled myself, a squelchy mess in my pants. I walked all the way home with my pants full of shit, breakfast and lunch; I was caked in it. Running down the insides of my legs, into my socks, I smelt like shit.

I arrived home. No hello, nothing like that. Boris had just finished an early shift. I know this because he was in the bath; it would have been around 3 p.m. The next thing I remember—and this is a memory clear as the driven snow I'm sitting in a bath of cold, dirty water. His dirty bath water covered in shit, covered head to toe in shit.

She left me there for the best part of an hour. By the time she pulled me from the swamp-infested, putrid bathwater, I must have had early systems of hypothermia and dysentery. I was wrapped in something resembling a towel and left in front of the coal fire, shaking uncontrollably.

Earlier I wrote that I don't do baths, and that is one reason. But there's another reason: soap. There were no fancy products back then, in that crumbling rat infested shit hole like you have today that I experienced. Soap made from whale flesh or whale oil is a smell you don't forget. It was most likely in every school back in the seventies and eighties, accompanied by tracing paper for bog roll. Wipe your ass, and it's halfway up your back.

Today I've heard it's good for you. "Great for your skin," they say. But it's not good for you if it is rammed up your ass. Not for a small child with constipation, not good at all. So, unless I am missing out on something here, maybe a Mr's Beeton's remedy in the good housekeeping guide in one of her many cookbooks for small children, then I guess it's some sort of twisted, medieval, Wicked-Witch-of-the-West thing to do.

Constipation is caused by a poor diet with not enough fibre, fruit, vegetables or eating too much cardboard. Knowing today how twisted and tormented Doris and her mother were and are, it most likely started with a phone call to SS headquarters from the pay phone on the corner of the street.

"He's been constipated for a while now. What do you suggest?" Doris is having a confab with the SS leader who didn't want me anywhere near her gestapo bunker when Doris first took me there.

"Constipation is it?" Nanny Phillis is most likely thinking, *what sick and twisted remedy can I conjure up?* Bingo! "Have you tried inserting a bar of soap up his bum?" Now why didn't Doris consult with our GP or take me to A&E if it was that bad, a child laxative, or maybe a telephone conversation with someone less twisted, like my auntie.

The smallest slightest incident or thing can trigger a flashback which can transport you back to that very moment. You don't have to believe it, it's true. What triggers this memory, is a bath, a fucking bath. I'm led into the bathroom. The bath was downstairs, near the kitchen. I remember because the radio was on, and the radio was always kept in the kitchen. Until one-time 'King Kong' Boris launched it up the garden, kind of a radio vacation outdoors for the electrical device.

The pain was excruciating, more painful than any hiding I had experienced, white pain. As a bit of a plonker, in my late twenties and early thirties, anyone who knew me, knew I was mad for snowboarding, aka the astronaut, with such an extreme sport, that I loved, come consequences, such as concussions, sprains, broken bones, and in extreme cases, death.

If you've broken a collarbone, you'll know what white pain is. It's decapitation with your head still attached to your body. Not for kids. It stung, it stung so bad it felt like I had a dozen hornets in my arse. Tears poured from my eyes, but I was unable to make a sound as I had lost my breath. I had rigor mortis; I was being soap raped. This wasn't some old housewife's remedy for constipation. This was torture at the highest level. A nice soak in the bath after a hard day's work listening to my favourite eighties band playing in the background, nice smelly candles, you can fuck right off.

The odd thing was, for several days after this back breaking, monstrosity of a soap raping, every time I farted, several bubbles came out my baby bottom.

RACISTS EVERYWHERE

Even at the highest levels of management, executive
management, there are racists, its just another thing
we must deal with when we are at the top.
"Fuck me chef does like to talk after a few beers and a bottle
of vino, I know throw a banana at him see what happens".
You're an absolute wanker, I wouldn't have expected that from
GM. I would have expected more from you, but its obvious
you have a big mouth and are in fact a racist wanker. "What's
happened guys"? Why has chef left the table? "Someone,
I will not say who, wanted to throw a banana at him".

WELCOME TO THE WORLD OF COOKING PART 1: A CHEF'S INTRODUCTION.

I t's not the easiest thing, adapting to the outside world when you've had the wind constantly knocked out of your sails for the past decade. "Wipe that smile off your face, or I'll wipe it off for you." "Why are you so fucking happy?" "If you don't stop crying, I'll give you something to cry for."

So, in a nutshell, was I ready for the outside world? No, I wasn't. I had been enrolled at college at a young age; 15, it was just how my birthday fell in the year. During the first year of college, all students had to complete a two-week work experience placement as part of our studies to experience life or death in a working kitchen.

My work experience was at the prestigious four-star Opera Hotel in town. Every celebrity who stared in any pantomime in town stayed there during the eighties, and probably still do. I was mad nervous, proper nervous. I was doing well at my studies, practical and theory. When you made a good stock or sauce, or trussed a bird ready for the pot, you received good praise from your tutor. The more praise I got, the harder I worked. The harder I worked, the better my craft, and with that, my confidence started to grow.

Just a short detour if I may: I know I swear from time to time. Some may say I swear because of a poor education. No, the education wasn't poor; I just didn't get it. With my bullshit homelife, how the fuck could I concentrate at school not knowing what was in store for me when I got home or the mood of the household. It was play your cards right every other day. So, finding something I was good at and enjoyed meant a lot, it meant everything.

Besides, if anyone's ever accused you of sounding less intelligent because you swear too much, don't worry. A study found that those who have a healthy repertoire of curse words at their disposal are more likely to have a richer vocabulary than those who don't. Fucking great cut and paste.

My first shift began at eight Monday morning. I had all weekend to get prepared. I pressed my whites and sharpened my knives. I can't remember the specific dates, like a lot of things today, but this work experience in the winter of 1986 was going to be a game changer.

Monday morning, I was up early. I brushed my teeth, sprayed my pits, grabbed my clobber, and was out the door. No, "Good luck son," or anything like that. They knew it was only a matter of time before I was going to leave anyway and get out of their miserable lives.

What the hell was a, "Good luck, son," going to do for me anyway? This work experience would either make me or break me. Break me, and my future would have been so much more different. Wanting to prove my family and every scumbag who wanted to see me fail was my doing. It was going to be my ultimate addiction in proving my entire family wrong. An addiction where by I would attempt to take my life.

This is where my mind begins to wonder as I reminisce at the life I've managed to forge for myself, I can only smile. The guys I used to look up to, had the cool gear, the bikes, the family stand. Even the local shoplifter's, and the dead beats uptown were cool. The guys who would fight on Bond Street outside pubs and clubs on a Friday or Saturday night I thought they were so cool.

In fact, I thought every reprobate around town during the eighties was cool, probably because they were in their moment at that given time. I, however, was that lost soul who hadn't a clue where the fuck he was going. I just followed them, half the time getting up to no good. I started shoplifting, stealing bikes, stealing people's luggage off trains. If I thought I could steal it, I'd have it, and I didn't even consider the consequences.

I stole a bag off a train once with two other losers from a train station in Middle England. We were chased by the British transport police. So where do we run? Through a mile-long tunnel out of the station. We shut down the entire train service in the West Midlands for two hours. What dickheads. If we had fallen on the tracks, electrocuted, we'd be dead, hit by a Thomas the tank engine, the obvious.

It's a million miles away and a million reasons how I made it. Someone upstairs must have known a child born into so much carnage, and destruction might deserve an opportunity in life. I suppose it's why I use the phrase, "Kissed by God." Am I religious? Yes, but you'll never see me wearing sandals and socks.

I jumped on the bus, headed into town, I entered the kitchen via the staff entrance. This instruction was on my brief from the college's "First Day on the Job, back doors", I was greeted by the executive chef

"Change in my office. I'll be back in five to show you the ins and outs of my domain," he instructed me. The office consisted of a wooden table and chair, an ash tray, twenty B&H, half a bottle of whisky, dirty coffee cups, rizla, dirty chef whites on the floor, and a poster of Sam Fox pinned to the wall, tits out of course.

Starters, mains, pastry, pot wash, fridges, fire exit, my office. My first job was to prep broccoli for a function. Wasn't told which function, just to prep. I was dwarfed by six crates of broccoli. *No sweat. Let's crack on. Florets in the container, stalks in the bin,* I thought.

I practically stood outside as the prep area was situated to the rear of the kitchen, near the back doors. Within the hour, I was done, I cleaned my section and emptied the bin.

Now I didn't think anything of prepping the broccoli that quickly, neither throwing out the stalks, I just did it. A few more chefs arrived on shift and I was whisked around the kitchen during lunch service. I'm in my element, or so I thought.

The executive chef screamed across the kitchen, "Where the fuck are the broccoli stalks?"

Broccoli stalks, "Chef, I threw them out, the florets are in the prep fridge." Ever see a silverback ape on PCP? Yeah, a silverback ape on PCP with an erection. Well that's what this chef had turned into, chef Ramsey hasn't got shit on this chef.

If he'd said, "Stalks in that container," then I would have done the obvious. Now I thought the verbal abuse at home was bad, but this was on another level, another level on top of mount Everest level.

In-my-face, mustard-in-the-eye-sockets petrified, the ape on PCP with his lipstick poking out of his chef's trousers was going off. "Fuckin' bin. Get your black fuck ass out there, and get me those fucking broccoli stalks you fucking, spellcheck, gollywog." *Humm, gollywog*, I thought correct. "Get out there and fetch me those stalks you black twat".

The day had turned to a bleak winter's afternoon. Artic winds swirled around bins the size of a garden sheds. No recycling back in those days. Every department just dumped their shit in any bin. "Get in those fucking bins and get me those broccoli stalks."

"Oui, chef, yes chef".

Into the bin I go, full chef's whites—apron, hat, neckerchief, and so on. Within minutes I was frozen to the bone; believe me, there wasn't much meat on me back in those days. Knee-deep in hotel waste, the smell was something else. I ripped bags apart, throwing out every stalk.

Before long, I was back in the kitchen a total mess. The broccoli stalks were covered in all sorts of detritus. "Good lad. Now get them washed and bring them to me in the sauce section when you're ready."

"Yes chef, oui chef, yes chef, yes oui chef"

That evening on the menu, cream of broccoli and blue cheese soup topped with garlic-herb croutons, finished with creme fries, and garnished with the classic eighties' garnish chopped parsley. At 6 p.m. I was told to fuck off home and come back tomorrow if I dared. I cried all the way home, destroyed, beaten black and blue, wounded, broken. Fuck this chef malarkey for a living I thought.

I arrive home battered. I smelt bad, proper nasty, hotel waste nasty. There was no sympathy. Why would there be? Snivelling like a child lost in Woolworths, I attempted to explain my day. "I can't go back there. This cooking thing is not for me."

"You better get your fucking ass back there tomorrow or else."

That's the day my future as a chef was set in stone. Those words, "You better get back there or else," was the only piece of encouragement I needed to get me out of that God-forsaken house.

First job the following morning was to melt chocolate and make garnishes for the pastry chef. Nuclear-powered microwave no problem, chocolate in two minutes. Not good, not good at all, black chocolate toxic smoke covered half the entire kitchen. Chefs and waiter's half choked to death, it couldn't get any worse. I went back every day for two weeks regardless, battered, broken, shattered, mentally and physically exhausted.

This chef was a lunatic, don't like my racist remarks? Go fuck yourself. Fuck, shit, crap wank, go fuck yourself. HR go fuck yourself some more." Human resources back then: "Go fuck yourself." Is this how all chefs acted, "go fuck yourself", in fact if you don't like it, go be something fucking else, and while you're at it, go fuck yourself.

THE MILLION-DOLLAR QUESTION

"Auguste, where do you see yourself in 5 years"? Well my career goal, to be an executive chef within a prestigious 5* hotel, like this beautiful establishment, with a Michelin starred restaurant in my name. I mean really, how the fuck was I going to achieve all that, being the maddest frog in a bag of a dozen crazier frogs. My skills set was on point, I had worked 2 & 3 Michelin stars but besides being a functioning maniac with the mentality of an anorexic caveman the only kid in the room I was kidding, was me.

WELCOME TO THE WORLD OF COOKING PART 2: THE DANCING CHEF

The bus journey to the restaurant was a good forty-five minutes if I caught the connecting bus from the depot. If I didn't, I was screwed, a two-hour walk. The fare wasn't a problem. In those days I had my bus pass, a freebie for all those on a welfare while at college.

The Jockey Club was a funky, renowned establishment that catered for the in-crowd on the outskirts of town. Big wigs, footballers, celebrities you name it. Winter 1987, it was going to be my second work experience from college.

I had the basic skills in my locker: bread making, classic cuts of vegetables—paysanne, brunoise, and julienne, as well as macedoine and jardinière—and butchery of all the basic meats and filleting fish. I knew the basic sauces and their derivatives, Françaises, cake making, pastry, waiting tables, and basic sommelier skills in all good City and Guilds fashion. It was time to jump back in and experience the world of hospitality again.

Up, washed, porridge, college-issued chefs' whites in my happy shopper bag. Unlike the endless selection we have today, once you washed your whites, they'd shrink. And if they had creases, they were fucked; a steam roller couldn't get them out.

I had my chefs' knives, college issued, wrapped in a tea towel–type binder made of the same material your jacket was made from. There were inserts for peelers, Parisienne cutters, a huge chef's knife, a filleting knife, and a boning knife.

I had a serrated knife for carving up work benches and bread, a turning knife and a steal which was as much use as a blunt spoon once you'd chopped the tops of your fingers clean off. But they were free, and they were my tools.

Of course, I had the *Repertoire De Cuisine*. You had to buy it out of your own pocket, but it cost peanuts compared to what it is worth today; it's a collector's item. I still have mine, under lock and key mind you, stuck together with masking tape and covered in every sauce I made during my college years. Any chef from that era must have one lying around somewhere.

I was out the door and off to the Jockey Club, I arrived twenty minutes early. I assumed it would be a good sign for whoever was going to show me the ropes for the next two weeks. "Good morning. My name is Auguste."

"Go fuck yourself. Only joking. I know who you are."

"I'm here for my two weeks' placement."

"Not another one", the receptionist mutters under her breath. "Sit over there. I'll call the kitchen and let them know you're here."

Another what? I pondered. *A cheese-grating wanker?*

There was a certain smell about the place, like a damp storage cupboard. There was carpet everywhere, on the walls, ceilings, downstairs, and up the stairs leading to what I guessed were guestrooms.

"Are you Auguste?"

"Yes, that's me."

"We've been expecting you. You're late." She must have heard my insides fall out my arse. First day at work and late. "Jesus! Only messing with you. You're early, silly twat. Come on. I'll show you where to get changed."

I followed the chef up the stairs and through a maze of twisted low-ceiling corridors. "Here we go, a toilet." I could have gotten changed outside in the snow for what it was worth. "Get changed and come down to the kitchen."

"Yes chef. Oui chef."

"Mr Conte is off this morning. He'll be in this evening, so it's me and you, chicken. We have a party tonight for 120."

"Who's Mr Conte."

"He's the head chef and co-owner. Okay, hot section, larder which doubles up for desserts, cold room, and out back, across the car park, dry stores."

"Cool, cool."

"Your first job is preparing chickens. Follow me."

I grasped my blunt set of knives and was led down a flight of stairs and into a room that seemed like a torture chamber. Hooks hung from the ceiling. There was one flickering light bulb minus the cover, a wooden butcher's block covered in salt, a leaking sink, and stacks of crates full of chickens.

It was fucking freezing, Baltic. Oh, and I forgot the two kitchen porters locked in a bamboo cage in the corner. Talk about hell's kitchen. This was it.

"Here we go, butchery section." Butchery? What section? are you kidding me. "You know how to prepare a chicken for sauté, don't you?"

"Yeah." Qui chef.

"Cool beans. Give me a shout if you need anything. I'll be in a nice warm kitchen doing shit for tonight."

"A duffle coat and some gloves maybe."

"Ha, ha. You're funny. Chop, chop."

Sudden thoughts of doing a runner out the back door seemed an option "Do legs, get the fuck out of here," *Apocalypse Now* raced through my head. But where to? Home? I don't think so. I was obsessed, addicted in getting out of that place.

I was down there for what seemed like eternity, hacking and chopping at these poor dead creatures. But it wasn't with the lack of knowing where to chop, where to slice, and what parts to hack off. I knew these fellas inside out—poultry half, breast quarter, leg quarter, leg, drumstick, thigh, wing, flat wing tip, two bone. The carcasses were used for stock. Halfway through the stack of crates, I started playing around, cutting up chickens with my eyes closed, popping out the thigh bone from the under-carcasses with a snap of my wrist. It wasn't so bad after all.

All the time I was down there, my mind was free, free of all issues, my childhood, my purpose in life, my identity, I hadn't thought about anything, not a single thing but my sixty new friends who hadn't been slaughtered in vain. They were going to be something special—coq au vin—for tonight's function and enjoyed by many.

When I went to take a piss, I had to sit down because my dick had shrivelled inwards due to the extreme cold. My hands were blue, my feet, blocks of ice, and my eyebrows iced over. "You all right down there, chicken? How you are doing for time."

"I'm fine thanks. Almost done." Almost done, and it wasn't even lunchtime.

Split shifts were all the go back in those days. You were lucky if you got out. I spent my first split shift sitting in the toilet cubical, ironically eating chicken and chips cooked by my new nemesis. After I finished, I just sat there wondering if I could get away with a quick wank.

Four bells and back in the kitchen. I wandered down to the slaughterhouse to check on my birds. The man himself—Mr Conte, head chef and co-owner of the Jockey Club—was already there, inspecting my work. He was fucking huge. I mean Andre the Giant huge. He didn't don the classic checked trousers and the jacket made of rhino skin. Oh no. He wore Ron Hill joggers, Fruit of the Loom T-shirt, Hi Tec trainers, and a butcher's apron.

"Is this your work?"

"Yes, chef."

"Did that lesbian give you a hand?"

"No, chef."

"Did you cut yourself?"

"No, chef."

"Where are you from?"

"Fire town chef, the other side of town, chef."

"Do you suck dick?"

"No, chef."

"Follow me."

He led me back into the kitchen, his stage, so to speak, where he dazzled many with his delights. I got a funny feeling that he had taken a liking to me, probably because I didn't suck dick. What if I did suck dick? Would that be a problem?

Maybe he liked my chicken chopping skills. It wasn't any of those. Mr Conte was a people person who enjoyed working with young chefs delving into his world. He wasn't a chef like you hear about today, a load of pan-throwing lunatics off camera. He was the coolest person I had ever meet, unlike those wankers I was knocking about with over the weekends.

He liked to show off his skills. He was a showman, and that night he made me sit and watch him dance around the kitchen for the entire service. This huge Italian chef singing, cooking, joking with the waiting staff without a care in the world—apart from his cooking, and he cooked well, really fucking well.

The following weeks we prepared game and offal, food I saw at the markets in town many years while shopping for the household, fodder for the weekend. The freshest of produce turned into beautiful, wholesome, delightful dishes. We cooked sole Colbert, sole Veronique, whitebait with lemon wedges, tournedos Rossini, steak Dian, steak tartar, T-bones and rib eyes, spatchcocked chicken. I lost count of the pasta dishes he cooked with what sauces and types of pasta.

I made potted shrimps and salmon roulade with the dodgy-looking female chef. Even she was a legend, she didn't care where you were from, what tribe you belonged to, your religion, or sexual orientation. There was something about her in those chefs' whites, something very attractive. The fact she could cook like Mr Conte was what was attractive. I indulged in all aspects of the kitchen, dressing the dessert trolley for the evening service, scooping out pineapples and filling the shells with the pulp and Chantilly cream, making all sort of gateaux's garnished with so many types of fruits and berries.

There was papaya, physalis, star fruit—the most astrological fruit of them all—mint sprigs, berries, toasted coconut and almonds, chocolate shavings, vermicelli, and glace cherries. There was nothing fancy about Mr Chef Conte, nothing complicated. Everything he did was done with simplicity, in fresh, cooked classic, garnished well, and served to the salivating customers.

He was the greatest chef I ever learnt from. My time spent with Mr Chef Conte for those two weeks was a time I'll never forget. A huge gentleman of a chef who took me under his wing and made sure my journey through his kitchen was one of joy and happiness. Fuck knows what happened after that. Must have been the war.

I returned to college two weeks later mad for it. As happy as a free-range organic chicken. I was like a pig in shit. I was hooked, buzzed out; nothing fazed me. I studied my repertoire inside out, back to front, day in and day out. I tested myself on the thousands of recipes, picking up kitchen French along the way, preparing myself for the real world.

City and Guilds 7061 & 2 French classical cookery, passed. Patisserie and baking passed. Food and beverage service for the hospitality industry passed. Culinary French terminology, all over it like a rat on a Big Mac.

DEMENTIA PLUM CRUMBLE

Hands down, if I'm playing a game of dice or cards today, the hand of all hands is going to be a full house, sprouts over plum crumble. I have no love in the world for tinned plums as I do sprouts, no love whatsoever. Bullet to the head or tinned plum crumble, bullet to the head, skin peeled from my body with a blunt spoon, or tinned plum crumble, the skin-peeling thing. Molested by a giraffe over plum crumble, the molesting thing.

"Okay, kids, it's off to your grandparents." Not my grandparents, fascists. "She's made her lovely crumble for us all. What a treat." I had two fingers to the back of my throat already retching before we've made it to the car for the journey across town for dog shit dementia crumble with cold, lumpy, fox-vomit custard.

No disrespect, but she isn't no Italian granny chef. The crumble topping resembled the glue you used at infant school to stick fairy liquid bottles together with green garden sticks to make a sail and gravel for sand. Yes, warm, gravel-type burnt topping with the gluey glop between that and the filling.

The whole dish was presented like a Joel Robuchon masterpiece in a battered Pyrex dish. We all had to marvel at it and then sit there and consume it like it was a warm, triple-chocolate fudge cake, with more fudge on top of the fudge, caramel filling with vanilla bean ice cream and marshmallows, and then fudge sauce poured on top. Garnished, of course, with sprinkles and chocolate wafers.

Fuck that shit. I was more than prepared to be at the table for two weeks. I knew Phillis didn't have a shotgun, so what was the worst that could happen, I don't get a blue ribbon for being a good boy because I didn't eat all my pudding? You can stick that blue ribbon where the sun has never shined. I'm a soldier in the making and you or your crumble will not break me.

WHEN MENTAL HEALTH SAID HELLO

The first-time mental health said hello to me, it was 2007. I was out in Australia with my ex-partner. Her parents had given us their holiday home for the week. It was a three-hour drive north of Sydney, in a small collection of exclusive chalets within a private gated area. The place was stunning. Her parents' chalet was proper bling, spacious, well stocked, all the "mod cons".

The first evening we settled in, BBQ and drinks, the following morning we walked to the local seaside resort which was no bigger than a small village, beautiful. It was no stroll up the garden pathway and a gentle knock at the door when mental health introduced itself to me. No, no, no.

It was violent, like a dozen bullets to the head, an axe to the face, a shovel up my ass, a skewer up my nose, boiling sugar poured over my ball sack, my spin pulled from my body via my ears. We had just walked out of a beautiful souvenir shop, and *bang!* The big bang went off like lemon juice and salt on the brain.

Anger, horror, murder, violence, rape, genocide, mutilation ran through my veins. I wanted to kill everyone in sight. I had visions of myself walking through that village and killing everything and everyone. Women, children, old folk, any who moved. I had guns, knives, machetes, the whole fucking shcbang playing out like some fucking horror movie while I'm walking hand in hand with my partner. "You okay, babe?"

"Yeah, I'm fine, babe." Fine? How far from the fucking truth, what was I going to say? That I'm the grim reaper on speed? Fine was me in a silk bathrobe, wearing fluffy slippers, sipping a nice glass wine eating smelly cheese watching a sci-fi movie.

This played out for the best part of two hours. Lemon juice in my eyes, nails in my brain, scotch bonnets lodged in the back of my throat. I was fucking drowning. I didn't know what to do, what was going on. I was scared, frightened. It was the first time I felt the presence of the cold, dark blanket—suicide. Killing myself would have been the easy option that day. Back to the villa, rusty box cutter across the wrists and throat, job done.

I'd just been brain raped, and it didn't feel good. The only way I was going to suppress this was with booze, loads of booze, until I passed the fuck out. Several weeks later welcome home United Kingdom, dealer, drugs, booze. I hid away for several days, several fucking days in a drug induced self-medicating coma.

Hello, it's me again, "MH2", Christmas 2009. I'm driving to Ipswich to be with my cousins, and it was the first time my future wife would meet my family.

Christmas Day, It's crisp and fresh outside, blue skies, picture perfect. I walked into the kitchen pumped for our Christmas breakfast. I pictured myself smashing my now-wife's face into the sink and cutting her head off with a carving knife. I sliced off both her breasts and volleyed her head through the window.

Yet again out of the fucking blue, *boom!* Scrambled brain and smoked salmon for breakfast. I saw myself sitting at the table and hacking at my cousin's throat with a blunt dinner knife, attacking it like some ravaged cannibal, writing "Merry Crimbo" on the table with her warm blood. I've cooked the little one in the microwave and hanged everyone else from the Christmas tree, there was peeled flesh covered in marmite and sprinkles hanging from the ceiling, on with dinner preparations.

Please, God, this can't be happening, what is going on, I've just entered the gates of hell on Christmas Day and my head was screaming from the inside. Black and grey shadows shrouded my racing thoughts. *Why am I having these thoughts, thoughts about hurting my loved ones, hurting the ones I love?* I was well and truly messed up. "Messed up" is putting it lightly considering my mindset.

It being Christmas, the only way to deal with this was to drink and drink I did, I drank like 10 men in Weatherspoon's. When breakfast was over, I put on my chef's jacket on and began prep. I had three large glasses of wine positioned around the kitchen in case I forgot where I had put one. Plus, a can of beer was open in the fridge, and there were the standard 30-minute vodka shots. When dinner had finished, I would be upstairs chopping out a fat lines of cocaine, which would just accelerate everything and make the thoughts inside my head triple worse, more booze, more hard booze and more cocaine was the answer. If I couldn't snort it, id fucking smoke it. If I couldn't smoke or snort it, Id eat it.

After years of self-inflicted abuse, I could handle my booze and drugs. LOL. Sorry, hold on. Handle my booze and drugs? No, the booze and drugs were handling me. When I came down from a session, my thoughts were on another level. I'd have thoughts and visions of walking to the local train station in the village, a five-minute walk from our house, and stepping out in front of the first train to Paddington.

Flying was a nightmare. I believed I had Goliath strength and could take down anyone, even a plane filled with passengers. I would casually stroll to the door, look around, pretend to stretch and yawn, and then make a mad scramble to open it. Fucking chairs, people, trolley dollies were sucked out. Then I would snap out of it, distracted by something, I would order several small plastic bottles of wine.

I mutilated my wife a hundred ways, I slaughtered all my neighbours in the most horrific ways. Burnt my friends alive, suffocated my daughter, and raped and murdered countless victims. I decapitated more people than I can remember, I chopped up and buried countless victims. The more aggressive and violent the thoughts, the more drugs and alcohol I consumed. The more I consumed, the stronger the comedowns which resulted in attempted suicide.

I wasn't only addicted to drugs and alcohol. I was also addicted to sex, porn, strip clubs, the whole fucking buffet. I wanted it all, and I took it all. Every fucking piece of an intoxicated boozy brunch in Dubai; I smashed the lot. To this day I cringe, I cringe at some of things I did and some of the situations I put myself in during those horrific episodes of total and utter madness.

To this day I haven't had the stomach to tell anyone—my wife, family members, closest friends, let alone psychologists or any of the doctors I have recently had assessments with—about the actual thoughts I was having for fear of being sectioned or considered a risk. Please forgive me if what you are reading has bought tears to your eyes, but these visions were the awake versions of my nightmares.

"But"—and this is no ordinary "but"—all my thoughts, thank God and heaven on earth and all above, everything I was thinking was passive. The slightest thought that I was in a physical state to commit any such acts of horror towards anyone, my life would have been the price, quick easy and painless, first train to Paddington.

What I remember most about those times I sat with my physiologist or doctor during one of the many visits to A&E for overdosing … By the way, there is a banging rave tune from the early nineties called "Overdose": It goes something like this: "Mr Smith your son is dead, how did he die, he died of an overdose," then the most insane break beat.

Apologies totally went off road there again. Let's try and remain focused as I would like to finish this project. Yes, my childhood always come up as pieces of the puzzle. The subject somehow, somewhere always came up, my childhood, I was in no state to put two and two together. How could I possibly put to and two together if two and two equalled 4 tickets, more drugs.

I remember I once said to Doris at a family birthday—I think it was hers—that I had problems with cocaine. She looked at me like a gold fish and said, "Sorry, son, that was never my thing" and walked off. Not a solitary member of that god forsaken family wanted to know my sickness. They would change the subject and empathize at a toxic level that sexual predators within the family were somewhat misunderstood. If I could write words down that could describe the disgust I have, "CUNTS".

All they wanted was to cling to me like leeches, like blood-sucking swamp leeches, so that maybe I would become one of them. A father with too many kids to mention, a parent who would do nothing and watch his flesh and blood beaten by other people. That somehow, I would continue the abuse that was a part of their heritage for decades before me. Well it didn't turn out that way, fuckers.

MIGUEL'S TOYS

There is nothing in this godforsaken house
and no child needs nothing

During the early years with Boris and Doris, my sister and I lived in absolute fear. I was just a child, but this was the age I really started to remember things. I can close my eyes as a man today and go back to how shit life was then, living in fear day in day out, not knowing what was in store for us pesky kids.

"Quick, kids," she would shout as Boris pulled onto the driveway. Well it wasn't a drive as such, just the front garden. "Your dad's home," she would shout, and we would literally run for cover. We would hide under tables, beds, in cupboards, anywhere we thought we were safe. Anywhere we could hide we'd fucking hide, and Mother would make it a hundred times worse. "Quick, kids, he's coming. Quickly go and hide before he sees you." This wasn't playful shenanigans. This was her putting the fear of God in us.

We scampered, terrorized, our little hearts beating out of our little chests. "Quick, he's at the door." The only reason I can come up with for this kind of terror—well, there are probably a dozen—but the main one being that she totally fucking resented the air we breathed, the ground we walked on; she felt total resentment toward us. The sheer sound of those footsteps walking through the house still sends shivers down my spine.

The love I have for my son & daughter is breath-taking. Every waking hour they remind me of all the beauty in the world. They remind me why I must be better and overcome my demons. *Love* is what defines us. *Love* is what holds our family together. It's what I try to embrace every day, regardless of whether it's a good or bad day.

I never felt the slightest ounce of love as a child growing up in that God-forsaken house. Every day was filled with screaming, domestic abuse, fights between her and him. Every day was misery, the house was infested with mice and rats running freely during the night. I could hear them scratching around beneath my bed. It was vile, damp, and depressing. Maybe we were the rodents living in their house.

The garden was always overgrown. There were trees at the bottom, we often built dens, me and my sister. There was also a waste ground through and beyond the fence at the bottom of the garden. There were slag heaps of old building sites, weeds, and boulders. During the summer, wild mint miraculously grew. As a chef, my favourite herb is mint. If I'm having a bad day at work, I walk into the vegetable fridge, grab a bunch of mint, hold it to my nose, and take a deep breath. It takes me back to the only time I found some sort of normality, scratching around on the wasteland at the back of our crumbling house, tearing at the wild mint, holding it to my young nose, and smelling something beautiful.

Most weekends, Boris and Doris left us to fend for ourselves while they went out. My sister would have been no older than seven; I would have been about five. Mother would put their firstborn as a couple to bed, eighteen months young at a push, and leave my sister and me to it.

This is how they rolled. They'd fuck off out without a care in the world, leaving two vulnerable children and a baby alone. As adults, my sister told me how, at the age of seven, she tried to deal with the baby's night terrors. Imagine that, a seven-year-old looking after me and an eighteen-month-old baby who brought the house down with night terrors.

It really hasn't been easy writing this. I've been tapping away on my keypad words, sentences flowing for the past few days, and I'm feeling physically sick remembering the neglect. My sister would panic, and the only option would be to bang on the neighbour's door, screaming crying, traumatised, asking for help.

"Where's your mom and dad?" the neighbour would ask. "They've left us. They went out," my sister would tell the neighbour. It was neglect on a scale that would have parents banged away today, well maybe not.

When Boris and Doris finally arrived home, they would be intoxicated. We would be punished for not dealing with baby. We'd be smacked about and told we were useless. "Useless fucking kids you are, fuck knows why I had you fucking pair, fucking waste of space."

There wasn't one night when I was a kid that I didn't cry myself to sleep. I cried out the pain as I shivered in a cold bed under an itchy blanket. There was no heating through the house, except for a shitty little coal fire downstairs. I cried until the world I was living in finally disappeared until woken by the sheer cold.

Some nights I would wake up due to the noise of the mice scratching under my bed. I remember vividly to this day I would get out of my bed with just my pants on, walk along the landing to mother's room, crawl under her bed and fall asleep on the floor. I was too scared to climb into her bed and ask for attention and warmth.

There were nights I woke up and the side of my face felt like it was burning, as if someone had slapped me in the face. I would be too scared to move an inch. I would be frozen in time, staring at the figure in the doorway to my room. I fucking knew it was him; I just knew. The fucking coward not only was it enough to be fucked over while awake, this abuse was going on while I was asleep. You're a cold-hearted bastard.

Back then, when I had knobbly knees and wore nothing but pants and a T-shirt around the house, I can't recall ever playing with toys. Our 'toys' were bricks and sticks. The one time I did have a toy was Christmas circa 1976. I was given a train set, a single track with an engine pulling a carriage around in a circle. I played with my Christmas present once, that same day, it disappeared.

The following Christmas, I got the same train set. The batteries must have leaked in the box throughout the year because there was silver foil crammed into where the batteries sat. It didn't even work.

A had a friend, Miguel, who lived a few doors up from us. I haven't a clue how we started hanging out together, most likely his mother babysat me. My friend had some amazing toys, including a figure of eight Scalextric, so many types of cars with a garage, and action men with vehicles. It was like Santa's grotto.

I truly loved being at Miguel's house, playing for hours on end in his bedroom. It was *Toy Story* personified. This is the first time I remember my first beating. I know there were others before this, but this was the first one I remember in my little brain. I always made my own way back and forth to Miguel's house. I arrived home after an awesome afternoon at his house, smiling from ear to ear, my face beaming as I walked into the house. "What the fuck are you smiling for? You better wipe that smile off your face before your dad sees you." Fucking dad. Hitler more like. The fucking audacity to call him my dad. He was a bully who preyed on me and my sister.

He walked into the living room, stood next to Doris, and asked why I was smiling and so cheerful. She asked me, "Did you have a nice time?"

"Yes, I loved it. He's got so many toys. We played and drank squash. It was awesome."

She asked in a sarcastic tone, "Would you like to live with your friend?"

"Yes. Just because he has nice toys."

"Well, you've asked for it now." I was dragged upstairs by that man. I was stripped naked and beaten, fucking beaten. My sister could hear my screams and cries for help in the garden. Doris was nowhere to be seen. That evil woman didn't raise a finger to protect me; she stood by and let it all happen. Raise me as one of his own? It makes me laugh out loud today. "One of his own"—the hatred that filled that dungeon was like a 2nd world war concentration camp.

A week later I was back at Miguel's house. I strolled down the road on my way home, wearing a gleaming smile. I'm convinced they were waiting for me because as I entered the house, I was summoned to the kitchen and asked the same question.

My answer was the same. Yes, I would love to live with my friend. Boris told me to go upstairs and strip naked. My sister was in the kitchen, kicking, yelling, screaming, "Don't you touch him. Don't you lay a finger on him, or else I will run away." This went on for some time. I could clearly hear my sister desperately pleading with Doris to help me.

While my sister was pleading with her, upstairs I cowered behind the door in my pants, petrified, shaking, whimpering. I knew only one thing: I was minutes away from another beating. But he never came upstairs that afternoon. My sister had saved me. She saved me today, but who knew what was in store the following day.

What I've failed to understand is why she went through so much trouble to get me back from my previous abusers. Once my wounds had healed from one experience, I was then "battered black and blue again".

There isn't much in life that I hate. I love my wife and children; that's a given. I love diversity, my profession, all sports, music, the arts, fashion, political debate, music, good wine, socializing with friends, eating out, golf, keeping fit.

I would say there wasn't much I disliked until I started this project. I won't go as far as calling it hatred; it was more like disgust. Do I have closure knowing he's no longer here, that he's dead in the ground? No. In a strange way, no. I don't have a clue why but for some strange reason, I still remember his birthday.

HELD AT GUNPOINT

During my years within the military, which is explained in more depth further on, I achieved a lot, did a lot, been there, done that a lot more. For the life and soul of me, I never would have imagined I would be held at gunpoint by friendlies, by my own.

It was obvious that recreational drugs where rife throughout the club scene. Anywhere there was a scene there were drugs, and the drug of choice for me and thousands of others was ecstasy.

The club scene in Germany was off the chart bonkers—techno, trance, queer house, techno house with some of the best European DJs spinning the finest tunes every weekend. So, what do you think a load of bored squaddies are going to do when they are off duty for the weekend? You guessed it. Get there rocks off; inexpensive, clean, and plentiful drugs; and go rave it up for forty-eight hours. We fucking loved it. It wasn't long before the brass across Germany suspected something wasn't all that it was supposed to be. They just didn't believe soldiers were getting truly and utterly smashed on fun drugs. "Lights out chap's, up early in the morning for more standing by your beds", I don't think so.

Beautiful, organised carnage every other weekend, coming back from raves thirty minutes before the start of my shift pinged off my eyeballs. It was easier when we were young. You just dug deep and cracked on with it with the least amount of eye contact possible. The youth of today go out, have a few beers, sniff a bit, and call sick for a week. Lightweights. Not that this is a competition.

In 1992, the biggest rave was hosted at the Olympic ice rink in

Koln, Germany. More than twenty thousand ravers were there to enjoy the hottest line-up of DJs. We rocked up mad for this rave, mad for it and it didn't disappoint. It was epic, the best rave hands down, twelve hours of bliss. Little did we know that across Germany, military police were getting ready for the biggest drugs arrest's in history.

We departed Koln in the late hours of the morning and headed back to camp. The five of us in the car were sniffing poppers and munching pills all the way home, buzzing. We drove into town, music blaring, we pulled up to the gates having half-heartedly tried to sort out our melons.

The gate swung open, a dozen military police, guns were cocked, and all aimed on us. *Fuck me. What the fuck is this shit?* I wondered, one MP shouted, "Hands up." Picture five smashed squaddies with their hands up in a car.

Another MP shouted, "Please step out of the fucking vehicle. Make your way to that wall and spread 'em." All the while we have loaded SLRs pointed at us. These cats were ready to do a job on us. It's not every day a soldier gets to fire off his weapon, let alone on guard duty in the barracks. 7.62m round travels 1450meters per second, it will kill an elephant a mile away. I guess we were fucking mincemeat if they'd have gone trigger happy.

What a head rush, we all stumbled to the wall, music still pumping threw our veins, legs stretched, arms in the air, ready to be searched. I know I had nothing on me, no weed, pills, or coke. I smoked and popped everything way before we reached camp.

We are searched while being screamed at. "You horrible little wankers! What the fuck are you supposed to be, 'gangsters'?" The car was searched, all the MPs found were a dozen bottles of poppers in the boot. "Right. Guard room, now!"

I had a good friend on guard room duty that day. As I walked past him, he whispered, "Refuse the piss test. Now this friend of mine was no ordinary friend. In 1989, I saved his life, yes, correct, it was I who prevented this soldier from departing the land of the living.

The stupid fucker was walking home pissed one night from the local nightclub, proper army pissed, there is no comparison how people get pissed today compared how soldiers drank way back then, there just isn't. He staggered past the only pub in town with a Turkish hit squad inside, enjoying their evening, singing Turkish songs about shagging donkeys as boys. He banged on the pub's window and shouted, "Come on, England! Come on, England!". If there is a bad move to be made in life this was is x10. Several armed-to-the-teeth death squad Turks swarmed out of the pub like hornets and went to town, I don't mean a slap on the cheek.

Long story short, to this day I don't have a clue how he managed to walk fifty-odd metres back to the barrack gates, get inside, and crawl to the guard room, where I was on duty that night. He had multiple stab wounds to his stomach, legs, and arms. This sapper was a pin cushion knocking on heaven's gate. His eyes were rolling back into their sockets, and there was hardly a pulse. There was no time for random chit-chat. I pulled several field bandages from the medical kit, along with two morphine jabs. In with the morphine and on with the bandages. In a nutshell, I was holding this fella's insides in the best I could. His intestines kept popping out from under the bandages. I was sure he was a goner; the blood loss was insane. I repeatedly shouted, "Stay with me!"

Several engineers joined me, working together trying to keep this soldier alive. He made it to the hospital alive, and miraculously survived the ordeal. So yes, he had my back that day.

In we go like convicts, heads down in shame. "Right, you, Auguste, first piss test."

As I walked into the room, I'm questioned regarding my whereabouts earlier that night. "I've been at my girlfriend's house, Sarge. These fellas just picked me up by the Commerce Bank. I flagged them down for a lift. I've got a shift in the officers' mess in fifteen minutes. I need to get showered and changed, Sarge. Oh, and for the record, I'm not taking any piss test. My missus will confirm I've been at hers all night." Okay, it was a bluff, but it worked.

"Well you better fuck off then and get ready for your shift." and that was that.

My commanding officer asked me a few days later if I attend the rave in Koln. I replied, "Not me, sir. That's not my thing. I fuck, fight, and cook, sir."

"That's my boy."

MARRIED TO COCAINE, PART 1:
THE LOVE AFFAIR IS STRONG

I n 2002 I finished a nine-month contract with Celebrity Cruises as a sous chef on a seven-day Alaskan cruise, cruising out of Vancouver, stopping off at Juneau, Ketchikan, Sitka, and the Hubbard glacier, which was very picturesque.

The entire food and beverage offering designed by the Roux brother, so being a sous chef onboard ship was a big deal. You were treated like an officer, you had privileges. I had to oversee all preparations and that dishes were served to specification during service. There were 3,200 passengers and 150 chefs. Food was available twenty hours per cruising day, so the output was insane. We worked seventeen-hour shifts seven days per week on a nine-month contract.

Once my contract ran its course, I flew from Vancouver into Heathrow to attend my brother's wedding. It was the wedding of son number 2 with Boris. Soon as I landed, I was on the gin and tonics on the train to Middle England. I arrived at Doris's residence wasted, put on my brave face, and went with the flow.

After a few hours' sleep, I picked up my partner at the time from the airport. We drove back into town, where I was fitted for my tuxedo, we shopped for a stunning outfit for my partner. Doris was divorced from Boris, so things at home were bearable apart from her excessive drinking, which she didn't hide, and her wicked tongue. The trick was not to get on the same level as it would only end in an argument, and you were exposed to the same slurs and verbal abuse I witnessed most days growing up.

Wedding, piss up, three courses, more booze, silly dancing, crap speeches, more silly dancing, fall over, Egyptian gymnastics, off to bed.

I had already secured a job for the coming winter, I was going to work as a freelance chef in the finest chalets in the French Alps. Snowboard all day, cook during the evening, DJ and consume drugs through the night. My partner and I had two months before the start of the season, so we decided to fly out to Italy and harvest grapes for a month. Best decision we ever made, though total bonkers. Up at 6 a.m., local breakfast, half a litre of wine, and then out to the vineyards.

Back at midday, another awesome local lunch—menu cooked by a demon old lady on the pans—more vino, and back out until early evening. Shower, change, another awesome meal, followed by stunning wine and a few spliffs. Winter season commences.

We drove to the Alps, set ourselves up in our tiny shared apartment, and on with the season, "twenty-four-hour party people". I was working at a very beautiful chalet for a wealthy executive for 70 euros per hour, plus tips and booze. One evening I was asked by a fella impressed by my culinary skills if I would like to fly to the Costa del Sol and look at a restaurant he and a partner were looking to procure. All expenses paid. Why not?

The following week I flew to Spain from Geneva. A hop skip and a jump, a short transfer, and I'm set up in a beautiful apartment overlooking the coast. That evening we ate the finest of meals, drank the best wine, and then off to the local disco, "skull fucked". Now this is where it gets surreal. The following morning, I'm stood in a massive, tropical-style restaurant with plastic palm trees, camels, and flamingos. The place resembled a plastic rainforest, very strange restaurant, run by Ze German's.

It was obvious the restaurant made a killing in the eighties, nineties, and early 2000s, but it was now suffering. The kitchen was a shithole. God knows how they did what they did, but obviously, they did what needed to be done. The location was bang on the beach. After an hour of over the head chit-chat in English Spanish,

German, and Geordie, I was asked what I would do if the restaurant were mine. I told them knock the fucking place to the ground and start again. After an awesome lunch, tapas with local wine, it was back to the mountains.

Before we knew it, I was back in Spain, looking at a shell. The restaurant had been procured, we built our dream restaurant. It had a huge terrace with an awesome bar. The kitchen was open, planned with a huge two-metre grill with all the mod cons, changing rooms, toilets and an office were at the rear.

My two partners were also friends with the financial backer, who hired a bar team from Spain. A week before opening, we all ended up at a beautiful nightclub close to the beach, a local club for the locals.

It was a very drug-free evening with loads of bubbles, banging tunes, and more Spanish snatch than locals at a bullfight. We staggered out of the club, hopped in a taxi, and went back to the villa. As soon as we were out of the resort, the cab driver turned to us and asked, "Coke, cocaine? You like da cocaine?"

This dude had been scoping the new restaurant. He recognized us as new venture, new money, new prospects, new clients. Before he said, "aine", it was an instant yes. It was a small detour to the gypsy camp, this was no ordinary gypsy camp, it was huge. Caravans were everywhere, it was like the stage crew for Cirque de Soleil.

Everyone male, or anyone who looked like a male, was armed to the teeth; AK-47s machetes were everywhere. Fires were burning in oil drums, and meat was being barbecued. It was like Afghanistan, but the driver ensured our safety and said it wouldn't be like *Deliverance*.

The driver popped out and popped back in, we had cocaine, a lump the size of a Matchbox Car, solid, 90 per cent pure. "No cash. Pay tomorrow. I come restaurant." Fairfuckingdincum, we just invited Pablo to the party. Talk about living in the moment. I'd just spent a third of a million on a brand-new swanky restaurant and bar. What's there not to love about life? How does the saying go, "Live well so we can fucking die well"?

The opening party turned a few heads within the local community. Restauranteurs, local businesses, clubs, and our new friend Pablo the taxi driver were there. A wise man would have known getting in that taxi meant the restaurant was flat on its face before we opened. You give the keys of your Aston Martin to a Welsh boy racer from the valley and tell him not to go racing, what's he going to do? go racing.

Everything we had in Spain was at the expense of someone else. For me, it was the party, I was so naïve, I lacked so much in life. I was irresponsible, immature, and totally inappropriate at times, but something in the shadows was there, it had always been there.

Growing up without a care in the world, just pushing it to the limit every day, some might say that's rock and roll. But the amount of cocaine we consumed started to consume us. It consumed us all to the point we didn't know what the fuck we were doing. Morning, lunch, dinner, throughout service, days off, no fucking clue. Apart from that we had wasted a golden ticket opportunity.

I was long-boarding "skateboard" to work in just my board shorts, barefoot, coked to my eyeballs. Smoking it, snorting it, washing it, snorting the stuff off gas cookers, tits. I was spanking a grand a night in strip clubs. It was the "wolf of Wall Street" on the Costa Del Sol.

I started DJing in a local club around the corner from the restaurant. The owner of the club frequented our place a lot as we didn't close until the last customer left, and most evenings we were serving until the early hours. We started chatting one evening after a few glasses of vino that led to a few lines, "Yeah, I can DJ", blah, blah, blah. DJing, nightclubs, drugs, I had it all. Life was utterly bonkers. Life was triple bonkers.

I knew there was a problem when I started avoiding my business partners and workmates to stay home alone, sniffing coke and getting off my box on my own. I had everything at my fingertips to educate myself and gain experience, to grow up and become mature and responsible. But I just couldn't grasp the concept. No matter how hard I tried, something was missing. Something didn't connect. It was the live fast die young mentality.

The restaurant didn't last more than a year after opening, we snorted everything. One year of cannibalism, parties, clubs, coke, parties, clubs, coke, hookers. I, we had lost the plot.

KISSED BY GOD

August 2007, I set off from Ipswich down the A12, heading for London. I'd just been appointed the new executive head chef of one of the largest hotels in Europe. Nine hundred bedrooms, two conference centres, three kitchens, and a staff of 160 would who require breakfast, lunch, and dinner. Then I had the guests to feed a top of that.

I was responsible for the entire culinary department, 30 chefs, twelve kitchen porters, a multimillion-pound revenue stream, and all the whistles and stress that come with such a huge operation. I nailed the interview while I was working in Dubai as a head chef of the famous Après restaurant and pizzeria.

The restaurant Après overlooked the indoor ski slope located at the Mall of The Emirates. It was a beautiful shopping mall with the world's largest indoor ski slope, a bonus considering I was made for snowboarding. As a chef, I didn't mind split shifts at the restaurant as I could get a slide in before evening service.

A 120-seater all-day restaurant, I designed the menus, trained staff on the style of cuisine, implemented all health and safety policies, and managed the kitchen from the front to back. I spent three years in Dubai. I travelled well and lived the high life as well as any other expat. I made some awesome friends, survived two car crashes, sustained a broken collarbone on the indoor ski slope, partied with celebrities, and dated a few models.

As soon as Après opened, we had the media all over us. Justin Bishop, the general manager, who sadly passed away years later, was a fantastic PR man. He put Après on the Dubai dining scene. When it opened in 2006, the restaurant was runner-up for best brasserie in Dubai in the Time Out What's On awards.

Into the third year in the sandpit, I realized Dubai wasn't doing it for me. I just wasn't thinking straight. I started acting erratically. My mind was bouncing off walls; I just wasn't me. I was ripping into chefs. I couldn't concentrate during service let alone on life outside the kitchen. I was losing it, my mind was shot to pieces once again.

A CHEF LOSING THE PLOT

"You fucking, stupid, homosexual, dick-eating, kiddy-fiddling bastard, felching motherfucker." Swearing makes you nervous? Holy Mother of God. "Do you fuck your mother or eat your sister's pussy? I don't fucking believe it. You're a fucking chef, and you're telling me that when I swear in the fucking kitchen it makes you fucking nervous.

"Fuck off. Get out of my sight, you fucking prick. No, better still, eat shit and die 'because I'm going to fuck you up tonight, bitch bareback. You ever made love to a man?"

"No chef."

"Well tonight is your lucky night, baby. Me and you in the dry stores over the tinned tomatoes. Yeah, baby. Hey, fellas, who wants to join in and make it a spit roast? Mumbles, you fancy getting your load off tonight son."

"Absolutely, chef."

"Put some music on. Let's boogie."

"Hey, guys", said one of my devoted chefs.

Bruce don't fuck with me, I'll stab you in the eyeball Lee. That cock-eating sausage jockey has just told me I make him nervous when I swear in the kitchen."

Silence. Then hell breaks loose, there are sounds of laughter and chanting in several languages echoing out from the kitchen into the restaurant. I can't believe it chef. Lame-ass bastard. What a pussy dhal-eating prick."

Then the inevitable happened, rug-munching, bongo head, "been there done that, I've been in this industry years and I'm only twenty-three years old new girl"— "I'm a proper foodie", who called herself the restaurant manager—stuck her head in the kitchen, and like some ponced-up Nazi dinner lady, "What's going on? What's this commotion? Has someone been burnt, cut themselves?"

"No, I've just chopped matey girl's leg off."

"'Matey girl?' Who's matey girl?"

"Oh, and for the record, I'm about to deep fry Bruce Lee's head in the fryer, and when I'm done, how about you step into my office and rim me for a minute or two before service? I'd like that a lot."

A typical and immature way of responding to a manager, but that was me. Losing the plot was an understatement. Now I don't claim to be any kind of psychic but the look on her face told me two things: She was either going to make the first and biggest mistake in her new job and stamp her authority down. Or she was going to pretend to join in and have a giggle about something she has no idea or clue about.

Guns at the ready, backed by a small army of knife-wielding auks braced for battle and a young sous chef eager to make his mark on his chicklings, we were ready to go over the top.

Taking a deep breath, I braced myself. "What the hell is going on in here, chef? Tell your chefs to pipe down and carry on with their chores."

Like a lunatic on speed, I unleash what can only be described as madness to the outside world, normality in an everyday working kitchen. Or was it? No, I don't think it was. The next day the manager resigned.

2007 I realized I had a problem, a serious problem. That ticking time bomb from childhood had started to simmer nicely. I had moved to Dubai in 2005 wanting to start a fresh beginning, live a good and decent life, and make some good money.

My life-changing plan didn't work out, I packed up my life, headed back to the United Kingdom, and walked straight into a job that almost killed me, again. My first year I was trying to hold down a long-distance relationship. I travelled to Thailand and Australia, weekends away. We stayed in stunning hotels all over the world, but it just wasn't working. The relationship I was trying to hold down literally blinded me to the issues I needed to sort out in my head.

When the mind has decided to pull down the shutter,
we turn into clowns, we are beasts without purpose
or reason, we are nothing, we are not even human,
we are empty souls waiting for the bullet. **AK**

MARRIED TO COCAINE, PART 2: IT'S HOW IT ALL STARTED, MY LOVE FOR DRUGS.

I was introduced to the drugs menu when I joined the military. Some of you might have seen the movie *Buffalo Soldiers*. Staring Juaquin Phoenix, a bunch of degenerate American soldiers up to no good In Europe. Well what I and my army chums got up to trumps that movie, because that was a movie, what us marauders "degenerates" got up to, was the real version.

The UK rave scene was well and truly underway during the late eighties when I joined the military. My first rave would have been collision at the civic Hall in the West Midlands. Apart from a blast on some poppers and a few larger and blacks, I didn't touch drugs. For me, it was all about the music and the skirt.

I knew a lot of people were on ecstasy because of all the gurning going on; there was a big old gurning competition going on that night. I didn't have an addictive personality "yet". I'm still fucking surprised I had any sort of personality at all during those early years.

Moving to Germany from Middle England was like walking on the moon. I was in the military free to experience everything. Free from mother and marriage number 2. I was fed well and paid well, and it was time to grow up and become a man. Well I don't know about growing up like maturely growing up, or even becoming a man, well becoming a man but not a mature man, not a mature grown man in any shape or form.

LIFE IN THE MILITARY: RANKS AMONGST STARCH-PRESSED CHEFS

P TE—*Private (that's me), same as a commis chef.* A twat who gets bested and fucked with all day, day in and day out. "Go ask the chef for a long stand." "Fetch me a right-handed whisk." "Go fetch the legs of salmon and elbows of lamb from the chiller." "Chop that flour." "Peel those peas." "Suck my dick bitch, eat shit, and die."

No one wants to befriend you because you're seen as a liability, a custard-burning moron. Your only so-called friends are the German dish washers, who are mostly Holocaust survivors who don't speak a word of English other than phrases like, "Can you pass me that pan please?"

One chef, who became a good drinking mate over time, used to tease the shit out of me. "That's the only pussy you're going get in here, sunny Jim. Imagine eating her pussy out—that one, the one with the moustache and the wooden leg—after she's been scrubbing pots and pans for fourteen hours in the sweltering heat." And like a stupid, pumped-up yank, he would shout, "Get some, get some. Go on, son, get some." I never drank the dish pigs' tea either, something about the slice of bread and the pickled onion submerged at the bottom of the cup always baffled me. Must have had something to do with the war, maybe nouvelle pot-wash cuisine.

Then there was the civilian butcher known as Bandsaw five foot no inches Bill, who left the army and married a six-foot Bavarian goat herder called Dave, a fine woman, the kind of woman who would probably tear you a new arsehole if you stepped out of line. But Bandsaw Bill always seemed happy, he stayed in the same job in the same barracks in the same town as a civilian chef. Not sure if he and Dave had kids; never did see any one legged gremlins around camp.

Bandsaw Bill went through frozen carcasses like they were softened butter. Blade steak, rib chop, sirloin chop, centre lion ham slice, spare ribs, chuck, shank, brisket, round short plate, knee chop, best end neck cutlets, chump chops, middle neck, belly, and bacon. The place looked like a fucking dinosaur graveyard, Jurassic Park 12, mass slaughter Texas chainsaw massacre stuff seven days a week, day in and day out, long before I got there and probably long after.

When Bill left in the evening, the place was always pristine like a surgery, immaculate. This old soldier had never heard of HACCP or COSHH, just old-fashioned elbow grease and a damp cloth, "old school".

Johnny Bing Bong, the Pavarotti of the kitchen, always sang Hitler youth songs. By the way, he was Hitler youth, still with the blonde hair and blue eyes. He was a massive old dude, six-foot eight. His hands were like wheelbarrows. His pastries, puddings, and desserts were incredible, out of this world incredible.

He always used to make this one dessert, simple beyond belief. He took bread dough and rolled it out into a greased baking tray drenched with melted butter, sprinkled it with loads of granulated sugar and cinnamon powder baked it until golden. He turned it out, sliced it, and served with Chantilly cream, cream whipped with vanilla essence and icing sugar.

He also taught me every swear word in the German dictionary. *Sclamper, arsechluck,* and *pimmel kuff* were just a few of my favourites. Great if you're taunting the Nazi locals; bad if you're trying to pick up a six-foot hairy German girl with a Chris Waddle hairdo down at the local Star Wars bar, not good, not good for morale if you know what I mean, seven shades of shit proverbially kicked out of you.

Every now and then, to piss off Bill, Johnny Bing Bong would frog march up and down the workmen's entrance, yowling Nazi war songs at the top of his voice. It drove Bill up the fucking wall. After twenty minutes of Johnny's Eurovision song contest attempt, it was party time.

"Snap, bada boom, bada bing." The most passive chef I've ever known turned into a psychotic, raving, five-foot, axe-wielding lunatic, mumbling, "What about their legs? They don't need their legs. Umm, man flesh. Meat's back on the menu tonight, boys," like he was talking to a small army of Bandsaw enthusiasts.

More yowling. "Mein führer, it's mine, a yar, yar, yar. Right left, left right.

From the butchery, Bill responded, "You fucking sauerkraut-eating, Jew-killing motherfucker, baby slayer, I'll slice your fucking face off if you don't stop that cock-sucking Nazi bullshit." And that was just for starters.

Once the rest of the chefs got wind of what was going on, they all legged it to the back, like trailer trash rednecks, shouting, "Black dude outside. Let's roll." They then joined the ranks, like SS madmen, with Johnny Bing Bong at the helm, frog marching up and down, chanting and singing.

"The show is almost about to begin. Take your seats, ladies and gentlemen." Curtain rises, and bolts of lightning, out flew Bandsaw Bill from his cave, carving knives for lung chukers, Mr Miyagi's roundhouse spinning-bird kick, tigers' claw, drunken master, wax on, wax off. "What about their legs? They don't need their legs."

"What the fuck?"

Everyone scampered, ducking and diving for cover in imaginary trenches and bunkers. "Come on, you felching faggot fuckers. I'll turn every one of you into mother-fucking spare ribs if you think you can wind up Billy boy. Now piss off, ya bunch of twats." Knives slicing through the air, Bandsaw Bill gave the Ninja bow of respect and looked at me. My bottom lip was on the floor, catching pork scratchings. "Welcome to the barmy army son," and calmly returned to his colossal cutting machine.

No one got sliced up that day, but half of the chefs were in the medical centre with concussions, abrasions, and sprained wrists and ankles caused by diving through doorways and out of windows. The master of butchery a black belt in pork chops and is a living legend, Bandsaw Bill. As for Johnny, the master of chaos Bing Bong, you will always be my inspiration when it comes to the pastry section. Quite ironic when you think about it. Ex-Hitler youth inspiring a black lad from the Black Country. I suppose it was never meant to be.

Finally, the local German porn star salad server. She was not really a friend, more like an object of desire. She drove me crazy every pissing day because she was a triple fit German bird who wore her chef's trousers so tight you could see her piercing when she took her apron off. Plus, she was the only girl I've ever known to pull off an Austin Powers haircut, this girl was unique, way ahead of her time, it was her who started my fetish for any lady throwing a javelin in chefs whites, buff.

I'd daydream endlessly of her knocking the granny out of me, that was probably why I was always cutting my hands to smithereens. "Concentrate, chef," she would say in the most seductive male / female voice.

The lance jack, same as a CDP. A total bell end, the sort of person I would smash the fuck out of if I were on civvy street. Basically, a promoted chef who just spent three years acting like a fucking schoolboy, arse fucking the living shit out of the master chef and everyone below him. First stripe.

Corporal, same as a chef tournant. Same as a lance jack but with two stripes, and he's probably drilling the living daylights out of some German model who drives a Manta. Duties include playing football, squash, tennis, pool, and cards. They get their own bedroom and have a dependency for anything illegal and have a twisted fetish for porn movies which include glass tables and dangle berries.

Sergeant, like a sous chef. Now these fuckers don't act like sous chefs on civvy street, Oh, no. These bastards are as fucking ruthless, right horrible cunts; evil, conniving backstabbers; my misery. These fuckers made me scrub drain covers the size of Tesco's with a toothbrush.

They made me chip all the black secreted carbon off the bottoms of pots the size of bathtubs that have been in use since the war ended with a tooth pick. I had to scrub the bin area every fucking other day and drain scalding fat from the fryers. If I burnt myself, it was funny shit to those wankers. No first aiders back in those days, you got told, "fuck off to the medical centre".

I emptied stockpots the size of metal wheelie bins, the ones that sit at the bottom of skyscraper bin shoots. They also doubled as pasta boilers, soup cauldrons, and when the steamer broke, a potato boiler. Cleaning one of those bastards just after you've had a stock going for forty-eight hours was a cleaning hell.

Twenty minutes of back-breaking, soul-destroying hardship, and there were three of them, I would be ordered to scrub out brat pans with my fingernails until midnight. Plus, on top of that, trying to kick out half a dozen stoned chefs with the munchies before you closed was a fucking mission. Funny as fuck but a mission.

An extra. One solitary, painstaking extra can be scrubbing the entire kitchen floor with a toothbrush. I had seventy-five. Why? I suppose I was the only black chef in the entire brigade.

The master chef, same as an executive head chef. Hardcore as they come, old-timers, Lenny MacLean's in their day, total respect.

I'd just come off a shift in the officers' mess and back at my dormitory, which I shared with three other chefs. I showered and changed, a four-pack and snacks I was ready to enjoy my evening. But before I settled in two chefs walked into the dorm—no knock, just bowled in and locked the door behind them.

Here we go, my initiation in to the army catering corps, the first of many beatings. How wrong was I? I will call them the two Dave's, I believe they had been keeping an eye on me from the first day in the kitchen, checking me out. Out and about around town in clubs, bars, who I spoke with, and what I got up to. But it wasn't much to be honest, I was still finding my feet. "Do you fancy a smoke?"

"Cigarette, yeah sure."

"No, a smoke. Do you fancy a spliff with us?"

"Yeah, boy, this is the army. Yes or no?"

So, I was on the spot. The two Dave's were different. They dressed differently, designer clothes, they grew their hair as long as they possibly could, when off camp they wore earrings. They both dated German women, drove nice cars, and were handsome fellas, spit roast.

What isn't there to like about these chaps. Do I go with the flow or walk out of the dorm? "Fuck it, yeah, I'll have a smoke with you guys. But I must say I'm a virgin when it comes to this shit." They grinned at each other and began to build. Cherry popped, I was as stoned as a caveman in a cave.

I was in with the cool kids, proper cool kids, I started wearing designer clothes I pierced my ear. I went to different clubs and learnt how to party, speak the lingo. Before I knew it, we were driving to Amsterdam and other exotic places. I remember my first trip to the 'Dam like it was yesterday. I had just turned eighteen.

England, Germany, Amsterdam. Life was amazing; it was fucking awesome. So, when in Amsterdam, you do what people go to Amsterdam for, to get bang on it, and we got bang on it. You name a bar, I've been there. You name a club, I've done it, red-light district educated. Name any type of weed solid, I've smoked it.

Purple haze, Thai stick, skunk, orange bud, Sputnik, pollen, red or gold seal, pineapple, cheese, white widow. Then came the main course—cocaine, ecstasy, PCP, crack, speed, but I stayed away from smack. My alcohol consumption went out the window, as a matter of fact there was no window.

You might be wondering, *What next for the skinny shy boy from the black country, full-blown gangster?* No, not yet. I excelled at everything, everything my schoolteachers said I would be shit at. Football, athletics, I was all over it. I played football with a famous Scottish footballer, now the manager of a premier league team. We played on the best chefs' football team in Germany before he left the army and went professional.

I ran for my division, BAOR (British Army of the Rhine), competing all over Germany in the 100 metres (sub-11 sec.), 200 metres (sub-21), high jump 2 meters, I was also a member of the fastest 4 x 100 relay team in Germany at the time.

Now here's the thing, I fucking loved drugs; I was hooked. When

I was on leave I'd be at any number of clubs in the United Kingdom—Hummingbird, Quest, Wobble, Digbeth Institute. Over in Coventry, it would have been Eclipse, I was smashed out of my eyeballs, buzzing like a kipper wearing clobber you couldn't purchase in the United Kingdom at the time. Before the army I was wearing old man's, clothes robbed from a jumble sale.

I was making regular trips to Amsterdam with a few friends from the camp, stocking up on everything. You name it we had it—e's, weed, hash, coke. We had the lot, and everyone in camp wanted a slice of the cake. Twenty-four-hour-, forty-eight-hour drug lock-ins, organised raves at the local nightclub, going to work high as a kite, driving all over town on acid, it was total mayhem, mayhem years before anyone in the military got wind of what was going on.

Then the Gulf War happened. Greedy ass Saddam Hussain was sticking his nose into other people's oil stocks, it was the flip of a coin which sent me to war, I was off to join the allied forces and take back Kuwait.

Hey private, here's a joke for you, "how do you stop five niggers raping a woman? Throw them a basketball", fucking twat.

CHEF'S EQUIPMENT FOR WAR

There is nothing in the desert and no man needs nothing

SLR—self-loading rifle, 7.26-millimetre rounds, 1450 meters per second; four-ton Bedford truck with enough rations to last six months; rocket launcher, dustbin cook set; number 4 cook set, twelve by twelve cooks' tent; four sets of nuclear biological chemical warfare (NBC) suits; 4 nerve gas epee pens; 55-millimetre Browning attached to the cockpit of the Bedford, a very big machine gun.

Before deployment, all soldiers, regardless of trade, had the chemical warfare menu. It wasn't a choice menu; you had all dishes, including the standard anthrax injection and the nerve agent pre-treatment (NAPS set). This war was different. Saddam Hussain was a lunatic, and he wasn't scared to use chemical weapons.

The number 4 cook set looked like a metal suitcase when closed. A little bit like a picnic table, you lowered the legs and then open out the table. There were four burners and a small metal oven which came separately. You just sat it on top of the burners; it was useless for baking. It came with two temperatures, hot or fucking hot, so anything that went in had to be watched with a keen eye.

The cook set ran on petrol, I filled the tank which was part of the contraption and pumped air into the system with a bicycle pump which would pressurize and then pass the gas through another pipe and out through the burners. So, you literally were cooking on gas.

Though a remarkable piece of equipment, it was a bastard to maintain and a fucker to clean. Rumours had it one blew up and robbed a chef of an arm. Mine leaked petrol all the time. I just filled the bottom with sand to soak it up. Fuck knows what would have happened if it went up. I would most likely be walking round today minus one arm and half my face.

The dust bin was an actual dust bin, but you placed a metal piece shaped like a doughnut with a tube up the side and then a chimney on the bottom. On the side of the bin you attached a petrol tank with a tap which would drip droplets of petrol into the bottom of the doughnut. Once the petrol hit the bottom, it would ignite "explosion" and heat the inside of the doughnut. When the bin was full of water and tins of food, it would come to a boil within fifteen minutes.

Army rations combined with a little imagination weren't half bad. Each box had a different menu. inside

A—Baby's heads, otherwise known to a squaddie as steak and kidney pudding. It apparently resembled a baby's head when pushed out of the tin. This came with mixed-fruit pudding (MFP), vegetables, dried potato powder, and oatmeal biscuits (which were magic for making porridge). You had to soak the bastards overnight as they were hard as nails. Forget about dunking them in your tea, one biscuit would soak up the entire cup.

B—Chicken curry, my favourite, although it didn't come with endless amounts of poppadum, mango chutney, lime pickles, and naan bread, this recipe came with rice, tinned fruit salad and a few other bits one being a can opener, no quick release pull like you have today.

C—Stewing steak which was great for making pies if you had a few fresh rations, which we did every second week—eggs, flour, pasta, herbs and spices, fresh fruit, and meat. Also, in the ration boxes came tinned luncheon meat, beans, donkey meat sausages, powdered milk, tea, coffee, and sugar.

D—I have totally forgotten what was in that cardboard box, but there were biscuits hard bastard.

From what I can remember, the first few weeks where spent driving around the desert with my squadron, testing out our gear. I was obviously along for the ride to keep them fed and watered.

Sitting here twenty-nine years later, trying to write this chapter, trying to remember what life was like for those six months as a nineteen-year-old desert rat chef in the thick of it 24/7, believe me I had to put a few bottles of vino away to complete this chapter.

I'm not going to write about death and destruction, it was inevitable and something I'd rather not share with you, but I will later anyways. I haven't a clue how I got to this point must have been the pills. Sitting on the end of my number 4 cook set one afternoon before the ground attack, which lasted only a few weeks, with the end my rifle stuck in my mouth, my finger on the trigger, safety off, one in the chamber, shaking and crying, ready to end it all was the beginning of the end, the first time I contemplated suicide, and it wasn't because of war. I just had the perfect opportunity to do it.

THE FRYING PAN

There are a few stories which stand out from the chaos of war. One of them involves a frying pan, a fucking frying pan. We had just set up camp. It was early afternoon, and I was stretching my legs around the harbour area when I came up on a battered old frying pan, in the middle of the desert. This wasn't a frying you could rub and boom, Will Smith appears, oh no, I might have been in an Arabian desert, but this was war.

This thing was fucked, It looked like it had been run over by an entire army. The handle was hanging off, and the sides were bent back. But when I rubbed the sand from the inside, it had a non-stick base, something rare in army-issue pots and pans.

I took the pan back to my field "desert" kitchen and gave it a good seeing to. I smashed the sides back as best I could with a spanner. Then I screwed the handle back and taped it with duct tape. Gave the fella a good wash and proved it with salt on my petrol burner. Then I gave it a good wipe with grease.

A few days prior we had picked up fresh rations of flour, eggs, fruit, and vegetables. So, after reincarnating my frying pan, the only thing I could think of which was fitting for supper was Spanish omelettes, a dish I hadn't made since college and one the lads would not be expecting that night. Most likely a wholesome all-in-one stew with powdered mash and MFP for dessert.

I prepared all the veggies and taking in to consideration I had to knock the omelettes out quickly, I precooked the vegetables. I cracked, whisked, and seasoned the eggs with pepper and got ready for service for forty lads using one non-stick pan. I also prepared jacket potatoes and beans.

It was around seven. The sun was setting, and boy what a sight is was, a huge red ball of fire disappearing beyond the sand dunes. One of the sergeants strolled over to my cooks' tent to see how I was faring. "Evening, Private."

"Evening, Sarge."

"What's on the menu tonight then?"

"Spanish omelettes, jacket spuds, and beans."

"Bollocks," replied the sarge.

"Honestly, Sarge, no fucking around." I opened the flaps "easy", to my tent and there to his surprise was my mise en place, ready for service.

Within ten minutes, all the boys had turned up and formed an orderly queue outside, ready for a feed. "What's for tea, sloppo?" Sloppo is another term for army chef, who served slop to his men.

"Spanish omelettes, ya cunt."

"Yeah, get fucked."

I strolled behind my number 4, cranked up the heat, popped on my apron, uncovered my mise en place, and started the show. "Omelette, eh?"

"Yes please, sloppo," he answered with a startled look. He turned and shouted down the queue, "Chef's really cooking fucking omelettes."

Three or four omelettes in, the pan was well seasoned and in full swing. The first two had stuck a little, but I wasn't going to give in. Ten omelettes down the line, and I was on fire. The burners were pumping out maximum pressure, and the oven was acting as a plate warmer for the spuds, the beans were bubbling away nicely. Temperature inside my cooks' tent, 140+.

"You're a madman," shouted one squaddie. "This omelette is fucking to die for." It would have been quite ironic if a Scud missile had fallen short of Bagdad and blown us all to kingdom come.

"You're welcome. Enjoy." The sergeants stood back and watched as I cooked, tossed, and served piping hot tasty omelettes to my fellow desert rats.

The sweat was pouring off me. My tent didn't have the luxury of extraction or AC, just a cool breeze wafting through my tent. After twenty minutes, I had fed all the lads, including the top brass.

I was so pumped and buzzed out I wasn't hungry. I just skulled a bottle of water. That night I didn't wash a thing or prep a morsel for breakfast the following morning. The old boys knew they had seen something never seen before during active service.

I received a standing ovation and a pat on the back. One of the sergeants came over and asked where I purchased the frying pan. "I found it, Sarge, over there."

"You're a legend. The boys are well impressed with their omelettes. They were expecting the usual."

"Not this time, Sarge. A few eggs, a chef, and his pan, and it's all gravy, baby."

"Less of the baby, Private. I'm old enough to be your dad."

"Yes, Sarge."

I don't know what happened to that pan, I just seem to have lost it. Anyways I hope it's with a Saudi or Kuwaiti nomad, being used for what it was created for, cooking on gas.

NEAR-DEATH EXPERIENCE

After the carpet bombing, we were well on our way to Kuwait A1 Escalon, just behind the main battle group. There was no hanging around. Most of our movement was at night, full power ahead, there was no time for error or school boy mistakes, this was war, you fuck up, people die, your friends die, you die.

Sleep deprivation and being in an NBC suit twenty-four hours a day was tough to say the least. My driver taught me how to drive the Bedford, hour on, hour off. This was hardcore trucking cannonball run with missiles, fighter jets, apache helicopters overhead.

We stopped for an hour, so it was un-pack the dust bin, spark it up, and feed the lads. It must have been midnight. The bin was full of tins bubbling away, A, B, C and D all mixed together a super stew for supper.

I set up a table with tea and coffee, milk and biscuits. I must have been two to three metres from the Bedford. "Fire regulations, hmm."

I stared to open the tins to empty the contents into serving containers when the Sarge came running over. "Sloppo, you fucking lunatic. We need to move this shit to the back of the truck now and quick fucking sharpish."

Chop fucking chop. I could sense the Sarge was in a panic. Three others came to help, and it was all hands on, moving my little canteen set. "What's going on, Sarge? What's the panic?"

"Just move, boy."

We dragged the bin full of tins and boiling water and the tables to the back of the truck. What happened next brought me to my knees.

In the distance I heard a rumbling sound, the earth beneath my feet stared to shake. All around me sand was being whisked up by the howling wind. The air was hot, and it was difficult to breathe. The rumbling noise got closer.

It was impossible to see more than thirty metres ahead of you in the darkness. Then headlights came out of nowhere. Moving at full speed, a whole squadron of Chieftain tanks sped past right where I had my little canteen ready to serve supper to the lads.

I was on my knees, watching in amazement, gobsmacked. If the Sarge had come over five minutes later, I would have been brown bread dead, splatted all over the desert and that would have been the end of that, no more pages to read.

IF IT HAD BEEN NERVE GAS,
I WOULD BE DEAD

Being on the move every day and night was really taking its toll. You don't really understand true willpower and determination until you're involved in a real-life war situation. Having to unpack and repack two or three times a day, off load and on load all your cooking equipment fuel, weapons, and rations in the wind, rain, pitch-black after driving hundreds of miles through the desert with multi-launch rocket systems (MLRS) flying over your head was truly a test of stamina.

One evening we had just moved into our harbour area. The boys had dug in, and I was still setting up my cook's tent. The wind was howling, and it was pissing down.

Trying to do this singlehandedly was mind-bending exhausting. After an hour or so, I had my tent up, but I was piss wet threw, shattered, and starving. But there was no time for rest. I had to get food on for the lads.

Outside of every harbour area a chemical weapons alarm system was set up. It sounds a high-pitch siren as soon as it detects any form of chemical weapon. The siren was so loud it would most likely wake up a piss head in the gutter in Bangkok on a stag do.

Tins in the bin, I'm good to set up my sleeping quarters, two dozen boxes of rations with a dos bag on top. Five-star luxury considering the circumstance. Out of fucking nowhere I hear a high-pitch siren.

WTF? This isn't the time to finish off a mid-wank while your eyes are watering with joy.

Military procedure states you have nine seconds to get your gas mask on, a fine piece of kit compared to what the Yanks had at the time. Nine fucking seconds. It's nine seconds whether you live or perish. Many of you might have watched *The Rock*, an epic movie in which bad guys rob a chemical warfare depot, move into Alcatraz, bad guy drops the nerve gas, his skin bubbles, eyes pop out, tongue turns into a three-piece sofa, his balls turn into popcorn then he dies a slow and horrible death.

Well I didn't get my gas mask on in nine seconds due to exhaustion and several other factors, one of them being I had my dick in my hand. Overcome with some sort of outer-body experience, my brain fooled me into thinking I'd just received an uppercut of nerve agent.

Gas mask finally on, I'm crippled. I have another handful of seconds to get into full NBC kit; it's not happening, epee pen smashed into the top of my thigh. I give into fate and except the fact that I'm about to rock up at the Pearly Gates or hell with two wraps of cocaine, a few crushed ecstasy pills, two acid tabs, skunkweed and forty-eight boxes of army rations and 20 B&H.

When I came to, I'm propped up against several boxes of rations with an epee pen hanging out of my thigh and my gas mask off. The Sarge was standing over me. "Private, are you okay, son? Son, do you hear me? If you hear me, nod your head. If you can hear me, nod." My head rocks back and forth, he takes it as a yes and demands that food be ready in 30.

PRISONER OF WAR

The purpose of the carpet bombing the 1st stage of the allied forces attack was to annihilate the main highway to Basra and everything in Iraq that resembled a military stronghold. The main command from Schwarzkopf was if anything moved, destroy it. This was the first time I had seen death and destruction on a scale that still has an overwhelming impact on me to this day. We had to cross the highway to Basra on our way to Kuwait, where we would be stationed just outside the city a few days before Saddam Hussain admitted defeat and surrendered.

I said I wouldn't talk about death and destruction earlier but the stench, nothing compared to it. The place itself cannot be compared to any blockbuster movie. I have seen the sun set in places which only tells me heaven is here on earth. I have snowboarded in mountains with crystal-blue skies which only tells me heaven is here on earth. I have seen beauty in the eyes of my wife and children. I have cooked stocks and sauces which have stopped me in my tracks. I have cooked and tasted food which can only be compared to great sex. Heaven is here on earth so is hell.

What we witnessed, me and my fellow men, those few days was something else. The sky was scorched black with smoke from burning oil wells. Cars, trucks, lorries were still smouldering, and the stench of burnt flesh and hair made your eyes water. Snap, crackle, and pop from fires still burning. Camels splattered all over what was once the highway. Bomb craters the size of Olympic swimming pools. When you have truly witnessed what another man can do to another man, your outlook on life becomes very different. What gets me to this day, almost thirty years after the first Gulf War, is the smell, the burning rotten smell of flesh.

We set up camp a few miles from the highway, my tent was up, my kitchen was set, and my bed was made. So, I decided to take a stroll around with my driver, helmets, body armour, SLR, and our wits.

We must have been gone ten minutes when out of the blue, out from a trench came one solitary man who had been hiding for God knows how long. Soon as he noticed us, his hands went up in the air, he shouted the only words he probably knew in the English language, "Surrender."

No messing around rifles with the safety off and a bullet in the barrel, aiming straight at the enemy, or was he the enemy, this guy was fucked. Was I going to kill a man today, could I kill a man if I had to? Yes, I would have put one in his head without even thinking about it if he had flinched or made any random gestures. Looking at that moment from the flipside today, if I had blown that guy's head off, or did I? Am I making this next part up, if I hadn't, would my life have been better, because it hasn't been any better, I've always been tormented. As he got closer, I could see he was wearing pink flip-flops—pink flip-flops, "bonkers" utilities and an army jacket two sizes too small.

"On your fucking knees. Get on your fucking knees, hands behind your head. Now." I might have forgotten to mention in the army you're a soldier before anything. That's what they teach you in basic training.

We bound his hands and took him back to the harbour area. We informed our sarge, who came over to my tent, "Fucking conscripts, Harmless bastards. Feed him, water him, and then he's off to one of the POW camps."

I dressed down and then sparked up my burner. I got a tin of stewing steak and beans. I gave the POW a bowl of water, soap, and a towel, and kept a close eye on him, I couldn't keep my eyes off him, it was weird, what was he doing wearing pink fucking flip-flops. The way he washed it seemed liked he hadn't washed for months. He was so meticulous. I'd never witnessed anyone appreciate something so basic.

When he finished, I gave him a set of combats and socks, sat him down, and gave him the hot bowl of stew and beans I had prepared. If I only knew then what I know now, a piece of Arabic bread would have been a treat. He ate all the beans and left the stew. "No like meat only beans, boss" so the fucker does English, cheeky cunt.

"Sorry it's not halal, mate." Fussy bastard.

When we departed, he began to cry. I could see the fear in his eyes, I told him everything would be okay. What could he be so scared of? I was to find out years later, after leaving the army, when the war was over, and the prisoners of war were released, most conscripts where shot dead in the desert on mass for surrendering.

The power, the force, and strength of the ground attack would have been too much even for a well-equipped military force. But thousands of conscripts were dragged from their homes to fight. Not a chance in hell my man, not a chance in hell against the biggest ground offensive of vehicles moving at one time since D-day, fact.

I have many other memories of the war, like the time I almost chopped off my hand and sprayed blood all over the kitchen on R & R, getting stoned in the dunes, fighting, drinking my own brew made from tinned fruit salad on Christmas Day.

Watching Scud missiles launched, flying over our heads during the night on their way to take out a tactical command centre, or a village or town. The Gulf War taught me many things as a human being, to appreciate life and all the trimmings, it taught me discipline, or so I thought. PTSD had hidden itself in the deepest parts of my brain, waiting silent, ready to pounce,

My co-driver perished two decades later, blown to smithereens by an IED in Iraq. Love and peace to you my brother, may your soul travel well for eternity.

When I returned to Germany, I received a commendation by the commanding chief of the allied forces for outstanding services during the Gulf Conflict. Many soldiers receive this award for bravery, aptitude, professionalism, and upholding military values. I believe I received mine for those omelettes.

My reputation with the brass was squeaky clean because I represented the regiment and won medals for athletics, football, cross country and the odd biathlon. I departed the army in 1992, when my three-year contract with the military had run its course. My military conduct was exemplary.

2007

I t was my first Christmas party at the hotel in which the woman I would marry twelve years later was also in attendance. One of the most amazing chefs I've had the pleasure of working with was also in attendance.

My journey with this chef will be kept private, sadly, he was taken from this world way too early, leaving a beautiful partner and children behind. May you find eternal peace with the angels my brother. There isn't a day goes by that you are not in my thoughts.

It's not going to be easy telling you this fractured part of my journey. It would require me to write another book, so, we'll dive right in. Cocaine is like Pringles, once you've popped, that's it, you're on the Pringle train.

By the way my issues with my mental health are still simmering on the back burner. To be honest, I've totally given up on that subject because now I'm in fifth gear, managing this beast of a kitchen.

2008, I move into a lovely two-bedroom flat and need to sort out a local deal as I'm new to the area, the quiver I've been getting isn't cutting it anymore, nose garbage. Who's the man who knows a man? Anyone looking for a nose in any London hotel knows it's the concierge team. A few phone calls and a text message, I'm hooked up.

I'm in, and this was where and when the whole fucking party went south, and I don't mean south like I've popped to the coast for the weekend or flown to Cape Town for bultong. If south was a planet it wouldn't be in our solar system. Work five days, get bang on it all weekend, back to work Monday morning feeling wavy. Work five days, get bang on all weekend, back to work wavy. Repeat. It becomes routine, and that's the killer—routine, work, cocaine, alcohol, work, repeat, repeat, repeat.

Before I know, it's the norm. This is who I am, a functioning fantastic junkie. I was still procuring my gear from the same dealer when one evening he said, "Listen, fella, you've been getting the £45 .7 nose buffet. Try this. It's the £60 .5 Bolivian."

"Why not? I'll take three." By the way, I'm earning good money. I have no kids which means I'm snorting thousands of pounds every month.

My routine took a turn, I started knocking off early on Fridays, just after lunch. I'd meet my guy; bang boom cocaine sorted; Friday Saturday Sunday bang on it. Wavy Monday. Tuesday I'm feeling ok-ish.

2008 is over, nothing has been sorted regarding my simmering stock of plutonium, carrots, onions and bouquet garni. My simmering pan begins to mutate into other forms of mental health and illnesses. Did I have a clue? No, I did not. PTSD became CPTSD, scarier version of the latter.

With cocaine comes an avalanche of other goodies, including extreme alcohol abuse, extreme addiction to porn, and sleeping with a multitude of casual fuck buddies with the huge risk of contracting all sorts of nasties. Believe me, when you're out there, and I mean orbiting some planet no one has ever heard of, the last thing on your mind is protection.

I was holding down the job but now taking risks, Mondays were a no go, and Fridays were a blur. I was having major comedowns on Mondays after a crazy weekend. I'd be sick as a pig on Tuesdays and have wavy Wednesdays. I would be back on top on Thursdays only to think about scoring my gear on Fridays.

I forgot to mention unless I was out on a Friday or Saturday night, which was rare, I'd be home doing all this coke alone. I seldom did it with anyone else, until I meet a crazy Maltese fella. Cocaine was my mistress, I'd I had become a full-blown junkie, that's a lie I've always been a junkie. Calling the ambulance was a regular thing, A&E was a regular thing, I was that guy you walk past in the street and say, "what a loser". But guess what? as far as I was concerned, I was fine. I was in tip-top shape, on top of the world, enjoying life.

The years started to pass me by, weight was falling off me like conkers from a tree, I was snorting half a gram per line. I'd hold up paranoid in my flat, curtains closed, with my boxers on at two in the afternoon. I would be covered in cream and feathers. Paranoid as fuck I kept looking through the letter box thinking I was going to be busted by a huge furry bunny rabbit smacked off his bunny ears.

Finally, hope, my future wife moved in, but I was living in denial, cocaine was still the lady running things in the yard. I had lost all sense of decency, all sense of identity. I cannot relate to love, I cannot relate to reason, I can't even relate to reality. I had overdosed several times. I was six foot three and weighed sixty-five kilograms. I was a dead man walking. I'm still ashamed of that person, that version of me and the things I did to my wife.

There are things I did that I can't discuss, but any junkie alcoholic will know the depths we slump to. Some junkies come back; some are still out there, waiting for death to come to them. I had lost the will to live. I had lost the will to be part of anything, without my wife being there, adíos to me, adíos in the ground.

Why did I want to die so much? was suicide the only way out, out of what, what was it that I couldn't grasp? What was I ignoring? Had the pot simmering on the back burner well and truly exploded? In 2013, I walked into my GP's office, broke down and begged for help.

The years between 2013 and 2020 have been the hardest journey I've ever taken, a journey back to life. A journey which literally killed me. I had to stare death in the face, and only when I knew the meaning of life, the *true* meaning of life and all its wonder, death would finally move on and seek out another victim.

January 2020, I assumed I was doing well, I was physically and mentally stable, but out of the blue with no warning came death and he came at his most powerful. His cloak wrapped tight suffocating me. I could feel my soul departing my carcase, soon to be splattered all over the motorway.

If the truth be told, I had slipped in and out of a few jobs, big jobs across the country, and the journey back to life was taking its toll. I had been in and out, and through the NHS system numerous times, prescribed all kinds of drugs, had more assessments than I can remember, and referred to various clinics across the county.

My OCD irrational thoughts were getting stronger. I was having frequent anxiety attacks. I was super-hypervigilant every day. My nightmares were off the charts, I thought I was ok, what a twat. On top of all that, I started to hallucinate without the acid. I hallucinated while walking down the street, in bed, in the shower. I was tripping without the LSD, or was it those tabs we munched back in the days, I don't think so?

While all this was going on, to add fuel to the fire, I decided to apply for Master Chef Professionals 2020, and that's was when everything intensified tenfold. My mental health went haywire. After two very successful telephone interviews with MCP, I decided to start practicing my signature dish. I'm sure you are familiar with MCP and the competition format. In brief, there is a skills test, followed by a signature dish, the knockout stage, an invention test, and another knockout stage. Then you cook for the critics, it's life changing.

I was invited for the audition stage in Camden, London. I was very confident and positive regarding the audition. I was geared up and in what I thought was a good headspace. All my senses and thought processes were super-intensified.

I was also in talks with a friend and in the process of setting up a pop-up food stall, Biriyani Bobs. Work was busy, and my food was getting mad crazy positive feedback. We were taking more private functions and bookings for weddings, birthday parties, and bar mitzvahs than ever before, and moreover, I was hosting a monthly chef's table.

On top of all that, I was at the gym every other evening, taking a testosterone booster, BCA, creatine, and drinking protein shakes. On 6 January 2020, I left work. I had already practiced my signature dish a dozen times in my head that day, but I needed to finalize the garnish.

By the time I pulled on to the M25 at jt19, my thoughts were travelling at lightning speed, I had no control of my thought process whatsoever. My thinking became dark, I was wrapped in a cold, grey blanket, and I could hear my thoughts speaking to me as clear as day. My breathing was erratic; I was hyperventilating. I felt a weight on my chest I could not shift, it was him, I knew it was him, he had finally come for me.

I told myself, *End it now. Just pull the car over and end it. Pull over and walk into traffic.* I could hear these thoughts in my head as clear as day. *It will be quick, painless, I promise you. Just pull over and walk into rush-hour traffic.* To say I was scared was an understatement. I was past scared. I was trapped within a cloaking force around me. I was possessed and needed more than a priest. The end of my days had finally come. But was this how I would go out, suicide, I'd toyed with the idea for decades, so why not.

This was the day I was going to leave behind two amazing children and a loving wife. I turned on my indicator light to pull onto the hard shoulder. Full beam headlights in my rear shone like an exploding star and the volume from the horn was like a nuclear explosion, the earth shock beneath me, my senses were on the outside of my body, lights flashing all around me, the temperature in the car was 20 below zero. Think of it as you wish, I believe that a greater force was at play that evening, call it what will, a greater power maybe, my guardian angel, I do not know. What I do know there is reason why I've written this book.

Decades of denial, ignorance, stupidity, drug and alcohol addiction, CPTSD, anxiety, years of being super hypervigilant. Years of carnage and damage I had done to others in my head, mainly loved ones. The destruction I caused upon myself finally caught up with me driving home from work, driving home from work of all things.

I arrived home in an absolute pickle, erratic vision, my head traveling at light speed. I look at the knife in the kitchen sink, contemplating if I should drive it through my heart. My wife knew something was seriously wrong. Quivering uncontrollably, I blurted out my mental health. Straightaway she was on the phone to the crisis team. Within minutes I was speaking with a crisis team member. I was on the phone for what seemed eternity before I came back down to earth, bruised, battered, somewhat lifeless, mentally broken, my mind in a million pieces like a smashed vase and a donkey was trying to put it back together.

At nine the following morning, I had my first assessment with a crisis team psychologist and psychiatric nurse. This was going to be first time my wife would hear the true extent of the abuse inflicted on me as a child and the horrors I experienced during my deployment as a desert rat during the first Gulf War.

This was the beginning of the end. This was the start of enhanced trauma pathway treatment and cognitive behavioural therapy (CBT) for adults suffering with extreme CPTSD. The non-existent relationship with my biological parents, with whom I tried so hard to reconnect, finally burnt out. It never felt natural to me anyway. Every phone call or facetime was an effort, I felt they were clinging to me for their own self-pity or for some sort of closure to the past.

It wasn't me who needed them. They needed me, those few minutes with me every other week over the phone, so that they might feel in some sort of weird, twisted, toxic way that I might have forgiven them both. 2nd quarter 2020, after lengthy consideration, I decided I had to let them go. For me to get my head straight and live life without distraction, I needed to do this. I finally plucked up the courage to walk away and turn my back on my biological parents, my terms my decision.

JUST ANOTHER COCAINE SESSION

An ounce of coke works out to be twenty-two or twenty-four wraps, depending on how much you are prepared to cut it. I went halves with a fellow chef, half for him half for me. Not sure what his plans were; I didn't really give a fuck, sell half, make his money, get high and try and fuck some bitches, I really didn't care I had a half ounce of block, not crumble or repress. Half ounce of crystal all to myself.

I left work pumped on a Thursday afternoon and drove straight to the off-licence. I picked up two litres Jack Daniels, a bottle of vodka, a large bottle of lemonade, forty Marlborough lights and cheesy snacks and headed straight to my apartment. My flatmate had gone to Germany, so I had the place all to myself.

Down to my boxers, I started snorting Thursday afternoon and stopped Monday afternoon. The flat was totally and utterly wrecked, fear and loathing. There was blood on most of the towels in my en-suite bathroom. Blood on the carpets on both sides of my bed on the walls, cigarette butts everywhere. A murky haze filled the entire apartment which resembled a Mexican smack den.

I'd suffered considerable blood loss, I was covered in moisturising cream, I was unable to speak and struggling to breathe. I was a dead man walking, death seemed to have walked straight through me. Death had been with me those four days. Death had always been with me. Did I care, no, so I chopped out the last fat line and collapsed.

Dancing with death, knocking on its door for so many years, willing him to let me in, I realised my efforts were futile. A bullet to the head would have sufficed. I had the one chance during the first Gulf War.

After those four days locked in my apartment, I came out of there different. Fucked yes, but something had clicked. The one thing I learnt was if I couldn't die, I'd better start living, hence my recovery. My guardian angel isn't in hell; nor is she in heaven. I believe, I truly believe to this day I hadn't even meet her yet, or knew who she was, or were she was traveling form.

SWEETS

One summer's evening back in the early eighties, I remember Boris and Doris calling us in from the yard, "hey kids who wants some sweets", sweets, fuck yeah. We only got sweets at Christmas or when we robbed money from the church. Like ravaged wolves we stood there shaking with joy. If I give treats to my children today I hand them to them. The bastard of a man threw the sweets to the floor, we went for them like dogs, like savages. I looked up to him, he was laughing, look at those animals.

THE RUSTY BIKE

That's what they called it, the rusty bike in the shed. I was never going to be anything to him other than his wife's mistake. It was all about his two sons, and baby three, a daughter, had arrived.

You would most likely think that all kids in the same household would be treated equally, but as you already know, not this kid. I was treated with so much disregard I would have had no issue with being left with my auntie in Ipswich until old enough to fend for myself at eighteen.

Our estate was weirdly odd, a weirdly odd council estate. I can't put my finger on it to be honest. We lived on the main road running through the estate. You had Flowery Gardens, where the KKK, Phillis and Teddy, lived. Thinking about it now, wherever we moved, they would move. When we moved across town, they followed.

Most family gatherings just ended in fights. Too much booze with way too many emotions, all of us witnessing the most horrific of fights amongst adults. For us kids at Christmas we were guaranteed WWE. Once Christmas dinner was consumed, there would be a good old scrap between Phillis, Teddy, Boris, Doris, and anyone else brave enough to spend the day with what can only be described as the most dysfunctional family on the estate.

I and half the estate witnessed my mother kick shit out of our neighbour years after this rusty bike incident; it was a proper grange hill scrap. As a kid I suffered with asthma. On a scale of 1 to 10, I'd say it was a 9, during the summer months, 10. Straight to the point. I'm out kicking bricks around with other kids in the large car park at the back of our house. I felt my chest tighten, it tightened so much it felt like a heart attack, or how I imagined a heart attack would feel, or as if someone had jumped on me and sat on my chest.

I managed to walk inside and using a sort of sign language, indicated to her that I was having an asthma attack. I was really struggling to breathe. There was no inhaler to be found anywhere. By the way, this isn't me slapping lipstick on a pig. This was how it happened. I'm now in a serious condition, wheezing heavily, every morsel of air keeping me in the fight.

What does she do? She doesn't rush me to A&E, like any other mother would do, or call an ambulance knowing full well they would have treatment for such an attack. She led me upstairs, put me on my bunk, and left me there. She fucking left me. My son falls over outside, and I'm all over him. Falls of a ride in the park, I'm there. On holiday, he doesn't leave our sides. Hawk eyes with tender loving care. That's me, and it was the same with our beautiful daughter.

To all parents, what would you do if your child was having a full-blown asthma attack and you didn't have an inhaler? Looking back in anger and disgust at the neglect, all the verbal, mental, and physical abuse, it dawned on me the perfect opportunity to use an asthma attack as an unfortunate death. I must have passed out as I do not remember anything after being taken upstairs.

Why else would you leave a child a child having a force 10 asthma attack? It's blatantly obvious they didn't want me, and I will leave this world knowing that.

The last half term before the summer holidays, most families across the United Kingdom are planning holidays. A cheeky week away before summer. I was out back with the rest of the runts, kicking bricks again about the car park. "Get in here, now." It doesn't take a giraffe to figure out this had all been planned out beforehand.

Boris and Doris have decided they are all going on holiday. Well, everyone except me. Now I wasn't old enough to look after myself, and I knew I wasn't going to Ipswich, let alone stay with the gestapo who lived on the same estate. No.

So, if I wasn't going to stay with any member of our immediate family, who the fuck was I going to stay with for a week? "Me and your dad are taking the kids on holiday," Doris said. He wasn't my fucking dad. I didn't have a dad, I had a ware wolf.

I didn't think there was anything possibly left for her to shame me with, but then came the triple-decker, shit, pubic-hair sandwich. "You're staying with Claire." Claire was our next-door neighbour's "grange hill scrap". I was ten at the time. I remember because that year I started senior school.

"But why Claire, Mom?"

"I'm not having this conversation now. You're staying with Claire, and that's that." That's right, staying with Claire for the week, speechless, mind-boggling speechless.

This was how low they were. She lied through her teeth. She convinced me that it would be worth my while. She and Boris agreed that when they returned, I would get a brand-new racer, a new road bike to cycle to school on.

Jesus Christ! A brand-new bike from the bike shop in town. Now any kid who had walked past that shop in town knew the bikes in there were top of the pops. I was stoked, proper stoked, over the moon. Okay deal. I'd stay with Claire.

They all fucked off to wherever it was they were going. The plane didn't crash because they all came home a week later. All nice and tanned, all looking like leather suitcases and all wearing fake Lacoste. Socks, T-shirts, shorts, wristbands and headbands, Lacoste lock fucking stock. Turkey! I knew it. I knew they were fake because all the crocodiles came off in the wash.

Why did I really think I was going to get a new bike? Because I was a child, and I thought this was real, a new bike. Wrong. They had no intention of buying me a new bike. I got the rusty dust bucket in the shed. Shame, shame on me. The piss royal taken out of me by everyone and all who saw me riding that piece of shit.

The laughing stock of the family, the estate and the laughing stock of school. That year both my halflings received brand-new bikes from that shop in town. While I've been writing this, I purchased a beautiful Conondale road bike. Cost a few pennies, but it's the first road bike I've bought for myself. No reason just wanted to buy a new bike.

IT REALLY DID HAPPEN

E ver sat in a stadium packed to the rafters and contemplated the fact that you're the only one there? Or sat in your own living room, wife nagging you to death, kids clinging to the ceiling and felt like you're not even in the room? Well maybe not because of the, "wife nagging you to death," but just felt you were somewhere else, in another dimension, another world, a place you haven't been able to figure out.

Haven't been able to figure out where or what or when or even how it's possible to sit in your own living room and be a million miles away, in another dimension, "Babe, babe, babe. Hello, anyone there? Knock, knock."

"Oh, sorry babe. What was that? Did you want something?", I've suffered with being distant for years.

I was asked by my physiologist how life was at home, how my relationship was with my wife and kids. Yeah, fine. We get by. Blah, blah, blah. But then it dawned on me. Physically I'm there, but mentally, I'm off somewhere else. I'm off somewhere else, trying to solve the universe's greatest mysteries. Nope, I'm trying to figure out what I've just missed in the last five minutes and contemplating why I've done the weeks shopping in Aldi wearing a G-string in high heels with a huge pink afro?

Until you place content into a blank space or thought of some trigger, you'll be out there in cuckoo land for a long time. My trigger was my sister. I needed something to trigger a process, a "Yes it did fucking happen"-type trigger. Or a "No, it didn't happen" trigger.

I spent years looking past things, through things, over things. I was seldom in the moment, never there physically, mentally or emotionally. I suppose that's another reason why I did so many stupid things, because I never thought it was real.

The period in question were the months, years before I could remember, remember the feeling of a shitty nappy, warm milk, being rocked to sleep or winded, being thrown in the air only for the person to step aside and watch me bounce off the pavement. Or how I became covered in bite marks and bruises as a baby. It's obvious I would have felt that pain, but I can't remember. Me being distant was me trying to take myself back there. That's all it was. No great scientific reasoning. I just wanted and needed to know.

I had to hear it; I had to be told it. There isn't a parent out there who is going to admit to his or her middle-age son that as a baby, he was thrown across a room or had his lunch poured over his head because he couldn't communicate like an adult.

My sister told me the state I was in as a baby. It wasn't good; it wasn't good at all. I'm not able to trust anyone, any family member today because of lies. The people I believe committed such abuse are no longer with us or hiding behind evil masks. Why would anyone own up to such horrors, most likely to protect the dead or keep the guilty hidden?

My biological parents will continue to hide themselves behind whatever it is they know, but they will not confess to anything out of shame. Over the years, they've had every opportunity to speak with me as I have been the bigger man and put myself in front of them on numerous occasions. Even when I was at my lowest, I had some sort of will to want to know why me, why me? and still no answers. I'm over trying anymore, hence why I've turned the page and moved on. My goldfish attention span wasn't because I was being an asshole or an arrogant up my own arse thing. I was just trying my hardest to understand what I didn't know, know about me.

ICE CUBES AND JACK

Another stinking year. Our firstborn was two, and I was in the darkest of dark places. My relationship was non-existent. Looking back, I hadn't a clue how my wife was coping with me until a few years later, when I started sweeping up the debris.

My wife was pulling her hair out because of the damage I was causing, so I decided it was time for me to move out. I packed my entire life into the boot of my car and headed to Ipswich, the one place I found peace.

I had been forced to resign from my current position, a constructive dismissal. I was paid three months gardening leave, so I had plenty of cheddar to see me through until I found something part time. I had also started legal proceedings which was also going to consume me as well as the hard drugs and liquor I was devouring.

The one decent thing which came out of this was my wife agreed at the time I could take our firstborn every other weekend. I'd drive south, pick up our daughter, and drive back Ipswich. I'd spend two amazing days with her and then drive her back Sunday evening or Monday morning. The only two day in the month I was half sober.

On the drive back, and every drive back, I stopped off to pick up an eighth of coke from a reputable dealer and a four-pack of special brew from the shop next door. By the time I had driven back to my temporary home I was wasted.

I had lost my job and was suing the hotel. I was slowly losing my daughter. I'd lost the will to function, and now I was dealing drugs. The inside of my nose was flesh raw. There was blood on every bank note I had in my wallet, and when I couldn't snort, I would smoke cocaine until my nose had healed enough to vacuum some more, which was approximately an hour or two.

My diet was also shot to pieces. A chef having worked in three Michelin-star kitchens and managed some of the busiest kitchens and largest hotels in the United Kingdom, I was nowhere near five a day. When I did eat it was ice cubes in a large Jack Daniels. I'd wake up in the most random places, wrecked and hugging a bottle of Jack with a note sticking out of my nose.

The meeting that should have never happened in my current state. I'd arranged a meeting with my biological father on the outskirts of town at a swanky restaurant frequented by football players, top brass, and bigwigs from the city. My objective was to ask questions, listen, observe, and mentally document. If answers slotted into those blank spaces, objectives were achieved.

I arrived at the restaurant first. I ordered a large Jack and lemonade and sorted the table. BF rocks up, smart, clean-cut. We were escorted to our tables and given menus and nibbles. We got a bottle of plummy red, and the chit-chat got underway. "So how did you meet my mother?" I thought the answer would have been more tasteful and somewhat respectful, considering I was looking for some sort of closure.

The dog shit that poured from his mouth was done in the most disrespectful and condescending way. A first-class cunt with no consideration for anybody apart from himself. "Son, I first saw your mom working at the same factory I was working at. Jesus, she had legs from her neck to the floor, a beautiful rack, and a backside to die for. Son, I said to myself, 'I've got to have a slice of that woman.'" By the way, he said this in a deep, believe it or not, seductive accent.

Second bottle, main course done, and he was still going on about his greatest conquest. I was gobsmacked. I just sat there, along for the ride. It was pathetic. Now regarding my current state, this fella didn't care the slightest bit.

Those objectives that I had sorted were futile. This man who sat in front of me had been doing what he had done to my mother to dozens of women. Now I didn't feel sorry for Doris. I really didn't.

I decided enough was enough. I'd had my fill of Mr Self-Righteous, and I had to get out of his face. We went halves on the bill, hugged, and we went our separate ways. On the way back to town, I called a dealer, scored a quarter of sniff, and headed to my mate's place to get on it.

I was strapped in, ready for the wave to break over me. I had no intention of seeing the sunrise. We sniffed, we drank, we sniffed more and more and more, we drank, and then I drove home to my air bed. I arrived home in six pieces, sniffed, had more to drink, and then decided dihydrocodeine and tramadol would be my cheese course half a dozen of each swilled down with Jack, Lights out.

A few hours later I make my way down stairs to the kitchen to pour myself a nice glass of chilled water. Feeling fresh and pallet quenched I make my way back upstairs, I open the door to my bedroom. As I slip into bed I feel the presence of someone else, I turn to look, it's me looking at myself sleeping.

I felt the slightest pat on my check, my eyes slowly opened. My cousin was sitting on the floor next to my blow-up mattress. She knew I went to see BF yesterday, and she was the only one who knew were my head was. "You need to come back to us. Please come back to us," she said. "They don't deserve you. Just let them go. Just let them fucking go."

Those words she whispered stayed with me, stayed with until I did what needed to be done.

A week later I interviewed for a vacant executive chef post for a celebrity. My résumé popped up on social media, and they were keen to meet me. I knew the set-up as I had taken my daughter there a few times when she was with me for the weekend. It was a busy place, popular with many residents from across the county.

The first interview was with the HR department. The interview went very well, so I went out and got smashed. I just couldn't help myself. The second interview, with the owner's wife, also went well, also so I went out and got smashed again. Third and final interview was midweek with the man himself at the farm.

The night before I had a few cheeky lines with a matey in town knowing full well I had to be in shape the following morning. Couple hours sleep, up, showered, dressed, and off for my interview. Fuck knows how I pulled off the interview, but I answered all questions and made some good recommendations to capture more revenue.

He was proper keen and invited me back for a cook-off. Seriously, I mean fuck. Third interview nailed, and they want me back for a cook-off to be executive chef for a shitty 25k.

We shook hands, he told me I'd hear from HR to schedule the cook-off. It was 10 a.m. I pulled out of the car park, pissed off, and headed into town for a liquid breakfast and to get bang on it. The place I found so much peace as a kid growing up in the seventies, eighties, and the best part of the nineties, I was going to die here, die a fucking junkie. A lot of people would have most likely said, "I fucking told you so."

During my 8th or 9th pint and into my 2nd ticket I noticed a missed call, so I listened to my voicemail. "Hi, this is Smile Hospitality. Would you be interested in a relief executive chef position in Shropshire. They are willing to pay £30ph until a suitable candidate is appointed. If you're interested, please give me a call at your earliest convenience."

The following morning, I had a short conversation with Smile Hospitality. I accepted the relief position and travelled up that Sunday to start Monday. The road back home had just begun, but first I had to sort out this kitchen. And it did need sorting out; it was a shithole.

The kitchen brigade was strong but lacked morale and a chef at the helm. Within weeks I had bought front and back of house together, departmental harmony. I had sacked several chefs, well told them to go fish. I had engaged with the sales team and regained the hotels 5-star health & safety food hygiene rating, plus bought all financials into line. These quick results gave the GM and the operational manager confidence in me and the team.

Its wasn't long before I was introduced to the hotel dealer, it wasn't Bolivian, but it would do, it got my rocks off and that's all I needed to escape into my own world. A chef with no filter propped up at the bar in my chefs' whites on ordering bottles of Don Perignon, thinking he's the man on top of the world, wrong.

Now that management had backed off I started to consume more olives and pickles, why, because they had just let a junkie into there house. Battling with addiction I didn't need an excuse, a pat on the back for doing well. Good day, bad bay, hard day in the office it didn't matter I was an addict.

The thing was, I wasn't the only member of the executive team bang on it. Anyone who has worked in the hospitality industry, either is or knows someone who is bang on it, using the quiver to get through there day.

I mean how else is the average human who isn't doing a 9 to 5, on their feet for 16+ hours without proper breaks is getting through their day? shredded wheat and red bull? I don't think so. The industry is in turmoil, If you keep your mouth shut and crack on with your day, achieve your KPI's, attend management meetings clean shaven, make the GM and the business shit loads of profit its game on to sniff that shit all day every day.

THE HAZINESS OF REALITY

The first time I met my biological father is the first-time thing which stands out the most. It was my birthday. I didn't have a clue what was going on behind the scenes; I was totally oblivious to what my auntie was cooking up.

The day prior I was out with friends. We had been out all day, drinking, getting high, and then we hit the clubs around town. Push Your Luck at the Caribbean club was on the menu that night. It was a shame what happened to that venue a decade later. The council knocked it down and turned it into a car park, a fucking car park.

Throughout the nineties, after-parties where the big thing. We got smashed at Push Your Luck and once kicked out, went on to half a dozen parties across town. I would be up for two or three days with ease.

Saturday night turned into Sunday morning. Most Sundays I visited my auntie, take my washing round, get cleaned up and have lunch with her; it was a social visit. She knew full well I liked the party life. I used to get juiced up on acid and speed when I was visiting while on leave during my army years before hitting the town. I smuggled back different types of weed and got everyone in the household stoned immaculate, proper, nice, warm, fuzzy stoned.

I left the after-party late morning, taxi to mine, picked up a change of clothes and my bag of washing, then took a short stroll to Christchurch Street. The day was amazing, sunny skies and a warm breeze. It was beautiful. I was still buzzing from the night and had been buzzing all morning.

I arrived at my auntie's house and was greeted with a warm hug and a kiss on the cheek. She knew I was flying, but I was never on the smack, so we were cool. Lunch smelled nice, roast chicken with all the trimmings. Umm, might not get much down apart from liquid in the form of alcohol. Cold beers were calling me.

My auntie treated me like her own son, and I treated her with the upmost respect, like a mother until she passed away of cancer in 2004. One cannot describe the loss to our family. We were truly heart broken.

I popped upstairs to the bathroom, before I jumped in the shower, I popped half an ecstasy tablet "green apples". I was just topping myself up, getting ready for an afternoon on the beers at the pub with my party people. Feeling fresh with a nice little buzz going on, I made my way downstairs. I told Auntie I was flying and asked if she could skip the main course and go straight to the dessert.

Apple crumble with custard. I passed on the crumble and swallowed the soft stuff. *Ding dong*, the doorbell rang. My auntie was all jittery and excited. "I've got a surprise for you. A surprise." Hey, a surprise. I rubbed my hands together. A surprise. Happy days! The gang had come over for a Sunday afternoon mash up. Nope.

My auntie answered the door. "Hi, come on in. He's through there." She walked this fella straight into the breakfast room, where I sat, having my dessert. "Hello, son, I'm your father." That was the first fucking time I heard such a phrase. "Hello, son." It echoed throughout the entire house, through my flesh, my bones. I was utterly and astronomically shocked. Where the fuck had this come from? I was buzzing and there was another buzz in the post, my senses had just been triple fucked, utterly triple fucked.

We hugged, more him than me; mine was more of an air hug, like hugging a total stranger. Well he was a stranger, I didn't know this fella. I was now in a state of shock and buzzing. He was talking, but nothing was registering. I'd lost the power to speak.

Battered, buzzing like a kipper, I said, "Let's go to the pub," and head for the door. Black Father Christmas and my auntie were hot on my heels. I set off quick, sharpish, and made a beeline for the pub, thinking about that first fizzy frosted glass of beer or maybe a nice fresh stick of wriggles and me not forgetting I was being chased by zombies.

The pub was packed. All my party people were cramped into the small beer garden. Pills and wraps were being passed under the wooden tables, friends were in and out of the toilets every five minutes. There was a buzz around the garden, it was electric, sun shining on every beautiful face. There were groups chit-chatting and smiley friends chewing their faces off.

I was handed a beer and a pill. I threw the pill to the back of my throat and knocked it down with a slurp. It was a beautiful day, but I was not feeling the vibe. Black father Christmas and auntie Stella arrive and join me at my table.

I was trying to keep it together when Johnny bent over towards me and whispered in my ear, "How's it going? How's it going? Really, how's it fucking going?" How the fuck is what going. He then said, "Stay off the drugs, son." That was the first piece of advice given to me by Johnny, as opposed to, "Would you like a bedtime story, milk and cookies before bedtime, a back rub maybe?" No, it was, "Stay off the drugs." I was on the fucking drugs because I loved them. It allowed me to escape, escape reality. I was doing drugs because there was something very fucking wrong with what's going on inside my head. It was he who was wrong, turning up that day was a bad move.

One of my friends asked me who I was with, and in slow motion, I replied, "This is my popohnny."

She replied, "That's nice. He's come to visit you on your birthday." I told her this was the first time I'd met him.

The beer garden fell silent. Half my friends' jaws dropped to the floor, as shocked as I was. "What a head fuck. What a fucking head fuck. So, you're telling me this is the first time you've met your dad?"

Yes, that first for me that afternoon was also a first for many of my friends. Apologies if that afternoon messed your heads up as much as it did mine.

My thoughts were racing. There was no control of what I was thinking. Thousands of kids may never meet their real parents, but when they do, they will most likely be better prepared than I was. I didn't know if I was coming up, coming down, or going sideways. I was coming up on another pill ready to blow my brains to marshmallow island. I whispered to a few friends, "I'm going to take a walk, get my head together." I excused myself from the table, kissed my auntie Stella on the cheek, shook Johnny's hand, and floated away.

I headed to the local park. I walked to the biggest tree and sat underneath it. I sat there until the early evening, staring into space and trying to piece together what the fuck had just happened. I never spoke with my auntie about that day. We never sat down and discussed the experience, how I felt, if I felt anything now that I had come face-to-face with my biological father.

I didn't feel anything. It was a blur, the haziness of reality, that period in my life, I found it difficult to feel anything, let alone love, especially the love for a man who had just walked into my life. I wasn't prepared. Nor was he. But he could have been, he could have really gotten his shit together and tried. After all, he knew way in advance he was meeting me. But at the end of the day, I was just one in a dozen of kids he spawned, so why the fuck would he come prepared.

WASTE OF TIME

When you've repeatedly been told by everyone you'll amount to nothing, put down, and be verbally and emotionally abused, something clicks upstairs. For me it was proving to everyone who beat down on me that I was going to do it, that I was going to have the final say, be somebody, but at what cost?

What was it going to cost me, really cost me? In January 2020, I was with my psychologist at the crisis centre. It had been about two weeks since my psychotic breakdown, and I was barely stable. The question, another million-dollar question was, "Why?" Why the fuck an obsession had become an addiction, and besides the drugs and alcohol, this was one addiction that was truly in my shadow all along. It was with me all the way, from the day I started my 1st work experience.

My kids and I were walking through Windsor on a sunny day. We were making funny shapes with our bodies and laughing out loud at our shadows. It was harmless fun until you think about your shadow and what may be looking back at you, what you can't see or touch or have control over is the spooky feeling within.

As I obsessed more about proving my family wrong, I lost all sense of why I was doing the things I was doing and everything I had done. I moulded myself so tight not to be like any of them that the identity, my purpose for searching, wasn't even within reaching distance.

I started living when faced with two end of line options. One, you end it here today, or two, you let it all go. Let what all go? Sounds simple, right? Wrong. When you've been addicted to something, something I didn't have a clue what it was, I realised at the precise moment everything I was trying to prove wasn't for me, nothing had ever been for me.

I wasted decades trying to prove to a family that didn't care if I was dead or alive that I was going to make something of myself. Sucker, that's me, wrapped so tightly I had been walking through my life blinded by the abuse I knew was always there until I had the balls to ask questions and speak out.

I suppose that's why everyone has fallen silent. They've all crawled back into their miserable, pathetic lives knowing I know. I fucking know. I stood so proud at my pass-out parade without you there. I stood so proud at every chef's competition. I stood proud when our children were born, at our wedding. Why? Because I did in fact achieve something, and I've got everything to live for, everything.

You may have wired my brain like a fruit kebab, but my dance with you all is done. Everything I do from this day forward I do for me, for my family, *my* family, my wife and children. You had your chance, I can no longer be shamed.

I've fallen and risen more times than I can remember. I've battered my body senseless, black and blue. I have danced with the devil, driven myself to the edges of darkness, and there's still one thing I cannot deal with today, no matter how hard I try.

Praise. When we praise people our kids, wife, family, friends, anyone—we release the feel-good vibe, a huge surge of dopamine followed by a smile from ear to ear. It gives our kids focus, motivation to do better, to achieve more, to want more of that feel-good vibe. But there is a flipside to praise.

If you're constantly putting your kids down, telling them they are useless, a waste of space, constantly criticising them, their brains have an adverse reaction. In other words, they experience downers. Persistent criticism breeds resentment and defiance, and totally undermines a child's initiative, confidence, and sense of purpose in the world.

Without a purpose in the world, I felt worthless. My only way to deal with this was to become obsessed with proving my family wrong. And where did that get me? Nowhere. Not being able to deal with praise has also caused issues in my life. I would respond to a compliment such as, "Nice chicken dish, chef,". There is no surge of dopamine, no smile from ear to ear. I just crack on with what I must do. And then came the criticism from others. "Did you see chef, how he dealt with that compliment? He's so arrogant, thinking he's better than anyone else." How far from the fucking truth? It's not that I'm arrogant, I just shy away from praise.

Or there's the subservient smile, a smile with no emotion, a smile to keep everyone happy, an obeying smile. I had a full-blown argument with my wife years ago. I was writing out Christmas cards and she said, "Babe, you've got such nice handwriting." She stood there and kept watching me write these cards. I felt so uncomfortable I told her to piss off.

COCAINE IN A NUTSHELL

First line 1988, last line 2019. Was it the ultimate love affair, the ultimate high? Hell no, fuck no. Would I do it again? I honestly do not have the answer to that question. The question I will ask myself is, Did I get away with murder? Absolutely.

Cocaine in a nutshell is nasty. It's up there with smack. As a middle-aged man today, when I do go out with friends—and it's not often—it was an excuse for everyone to get bang on it. WhatsApp messages back and forth weeks before the big night. "Have you called the dealer? I've got my tickle sorted." We'd all meet at a fancy restaurant. Half the boys wouldn't order as they would already be grinding their teeth putting beers away like a kid with a bag skittles.

Nightclub, I don't think so. It off to some skanky strip club, sat there for two hours talking bollocks to some fit bird from eastern Europe with a fake rack snorting ping off the corner of your credit card, asking the same question repeatedly, "Can I touch you? Please, just a little. Maybe a finger."

Still talking bollocks with a jaw at nine o'clock. It's a bottle of bubbles because she has persuaded you to spunk 250 large, "free bubbles". You get kicked out at closing time. You're knee deep in shit because you're broke as a bandit, and there are bills that still need to be paid. You arrive home just to jerk off to babe station, nursing a come down that lasts a week.

Would I get back on the biscuit train, would I do another hit? Fuck no, it's taken me the best part a decade to get off it, so I suppose that answers my question.

SUCKER FOR PUNISHMENT

Shortly after I moved back to the UK from Dubai and having legally changed my name for personal reasons, one being the fact I had the same surname as Doris's first marriage which didn't sit well with me. I had to rid myself of history and become my own man. I stupidly persuaded myself to contact Johnny, to see if he was interested in meeting with me. A good catch up was needed and for me to see what the man was all about, where he lived, what his life was like and to gain more understanding who my biological father was, and what he had achieved in life. This single not well thought out decision would drive me deeper into addiction, it was in fact the trigger.

It's a shame I didn't have such a wonderful phycologist like I do today back then, she might have said, "I don't think it's a good idea you take such a huge leap of faith considering you delicate situation", well shit happens, and the meet was set.

I decided to drive up north to meet Johnny, plus several of his children would be in attendance. To be honest I had no idea what I was getting myself into. It wasn't the smartest move, but like most other stupid irrational moves I've made in the past this seemed rational.

I set off early Friday morning with the intention of spending a long weekend up north with a family I never knew existed until a few weeks back. Thirty minutes out it's too late, I'm in the zone, off the motor way heading straight into the unforeseen storm. Why have I decided at this chaotic period in my life to be in his presence. It's simple, I want to be accepted, I wanted to know I was loved, I want to be told, that although they were irresponsible parents they both wanted the best for me, the best start in life so to speak. ""

The estate was a shamble's, it looked and felt wrong, apocalyptic, wrong like a war had just ended. I had a bad feeling about the next five minutes let alone felt good about spending the entire weekend here. If the shit hits the fan, well then, the shits hits the fan.

I've landed, passport at the ready for immigration control, this place doesn't look like England. I pull into what appears to be a car park, slash five aside football wasteland type pitch. I exit the car and head towards the beer jungle.

I was greeted by a dozen members of the family and their friends and the kids of their friends. Punched in the brown, kicked in the ribs, beaten black & blue, I hadn't even sipped a beer, my brain couldn't figure out what my eyes were seeing. Half a dozen clones, and their clones had little baby clones. A family of cloned half breeds, I need a line of chop to get my head straight. I'm tripping without the acid, hell comes to frog town and planet of the apes mashed into one. A foreign country surrounded by scary cloned people. This man's seed was atomic strong, even friends of the family looked like they had a splash of the man's genes.

From the off I sense something is south of the border, me, not only from down south up north. Finally, after decades, several of my half siblings have finally meet the man the child who without a doubt, one or two might blame for the mess they had to live through as kids, when Johnny decided to pick rhubarb from another mans garden.

The beers start to flow as I'm slowly introduced to the Harlem globetrotters, one by one. Being a wise man, and a connoisseur of the white stuff, it's obvious there's more devil's dandruff being consumed then there is beer in this drinking house. A patron has just exited the watering closet, it appears they have just stuck their head into a barrel of sherbet dip.

The conversation is intense, Peter and Simon a few years younger than me were cold. They were not interested in chit chat, small talk, getting to know me as such. They were in and out of the toilet playing some form of nose tag. Not happy bunnies, or the gear they were sniffing was nose garbage, not in my pocket, I've got the ping, the Bolivian flake. I'm not up for being responsible in giving anyone a heart attack today, so I keep my wrap for my nose.

Day drifted into night, it's warming up to be a proper cluster fuck of a gathering, there's a sense that someone has a lot of explaining to do. Four marriages, four sets of siblings and an army of kids and a bastard thrown into the mix. The mood changes dramatically, out of now where, Peter starts kicking off, in my face, "I don't give a fuck who you are Cus, no one here does, you're just a cunt, spawned from a one-night fling".

Tell me something I don't know already, I'm here because black Hugh Hefner needs to explain shit. Back in my face, "He fucked our mom over bruv, just like he did to yours". "Beat her, beat us, he's not a nice person cus, don't get to close for your own good". I take his words of anger and frustration on the chin, I haven't walked in his shoes, so I can't assume what I'm being told is, or isn't true.

The only half siblings that don't come across as cold are his two eldest girls, real nice, laid back and respectful to what is going on. After a few hours my head is an emotional mess, a sucker for punishment, I should not be here, my bad. I've nailed to many beers, I'm now on the JD's and lemonade, plus I've had two cheeky ones up the hooter of the corner of my bankcard, just to keep me in the fight, to see me through this nightmare on elm street.

There're tears, laughter, it's a crazy ride of emotions, but it's not long before the night takes a turn for the worst. Peter and Simon are juiced and buzzing their chops off, the other half sibling Marcus hasn't said a word to me all day. He comes across as a smug little wanker, there is nothing at all which I can relate too, all bar atomic seamen which connects me to this individual. He looks at me with disgust, like I shouldn't be here, he may have been bang on the money, I shouldn't be here, I don't belong here.

It's starting to sink in, that I'm in a world of no man's land, it's too late to drive 5hrs back to the shire off my nut, so I crack on and go with the flow as best as humanly possible. In a nutshell I'm in the wrong town, the wrong country and its Friday night in frog town. Piss heads, dust heads everywhere, and one fella with a foreign accent. The mood of the pub isn't a nice one, tension, beat up aggression, a pipe bomb ready to explode. The savage of all savages who's been eye balling me for the past hour with a strange head twitch from behind the bar, comes over to me, bends down and whispers in my ear "can you score some Niki Lauder me old fruit".

Gobsmacked with what I've just been asked, there is now another fella in my ear, who has appeared from nowhere, out the fucking blue, like a black genie. "You my brother from another mother, he wanted you here, so he could parade you in front of us all as his love child. Imagine that, all us lot being told you're his love child, while all he did was screw our mothers over. You don't mean anything to him, and I bet neither did your mother, how do you feel about that brother".

I leave the chaos of the pub, and sit outside nursing my Jack Daniels, why was I here, what was I looking for. I wasn't looking or searching for this detritus, tears run down my cheek, head in my hands shaking. I decide to call it a night and drive to Johnny's house, ripped, buzzing, pissed, peeled as a banana, without no consideration I was over the limit, there was no limit, just a broken, busted up addict, with no purpose.

I wait outside Johnny's place for an hour, Johnny arrives by taxi, come on son let's get inside and have a chat. Trust me, I'm in no mood for small talk, I'm beat, I'm off to bed. It must have been 3am, I'm woken by a loud thud, Peter and Marcus are kicking off in the living room with Johnny.

It's not nice what I'm hearing, it's not nice at all, these two cats have got issues and want questions answered, so do I, I have a ton of questions, but I guess it's not the time for my kangaroo hearing. Their voices fade, I drift off into a drunken sweaty sleep. I'm up early hung over in a strange place totally disorientated, not good for moral. I freshen up, black Hugh Hefner is in the kitchen, the only words from my mouth, I've seen and heard enough and leave.

I WAS THINKING ABOUT YOU

A year before, Doris explained to me that she abandoned me. We were sitting one evening in the garden, a beautiful evening. I asked if she had any form of security for later life, a plan B so to speak.

She explained she hadn't thought about yesterday, let alone what her future had to hold. I cut to the chase and explained she could purchase the house she had occupied for decades from the council if she wanted.

"Oh, that sounds too complicated," Doris said. After some convert station and convincing, we acquired the relevant paperwork and proceeded with the process. No one else had considered the welfare of their mother, let alone considered that a council house, a five-bedroom townhouse over three floors with reception, a garden the size of a five-a-side football pitch and driveway for three cars was worth anything. They all mocked the place.

Several months later, we purchased the property, market value was a nice surprise. She finally had peace of mind, they could go about their retirement knowing that they could relax and enjoy life. The house that brought so much misery throughout years she finally owned. She finally had security, something I seldom experienced as a child.

THE BEGINNING

I must confess it was my amazing daughter who brought me back. She gave me purpose in this world, dead or alive, buried six feet under, looking at all the miracles happening above my grave, brain dead, in an institution in a straitjacket, bouncing off four walls. Really.

There was only one way to go when my beautiful girl was born. Even before you came into our world, decades before I met Mommy, long before I was born. Millions of years ago, you started your journey across an ocean of stars and the eternity of space to help me through my darkest days.

I've truly danced with the devil. I wandered helplessly through the graveyard of my soul. I pondered for decades about my purpose. You were my guardian angel; it was you who gave me hope, it was you who showed me how to love, it was you who guided me towards the light.

My beautiful boy, without you this project would probably still be sat in the depths of my mind. Watching you grow has literally stopped me in my tracks, my little superhero, little do you know, but the light that shines from you and your sister has given me true purpose in this world, I belong to you and you are mine, always and forever.

My darling wife, I'm humbled by your forgiveness, I'm bonded to you for eternity.

My auntie Stella, I know it was you I saw in Ibiza and I know it was you who pocked me in the ribs at the funeral. You may have passed away many moons ago, but I know it was you I saw. I walked across the swimming pool area to make my way to the beach. No one else around, no one. You turned around to look at me and waved from your sun lounger. The halo around you was breath-taking, and the smile on your face sent electricity through me. I know you are in a good place. You were happy. You looked so happy knowing your two beautiful children and I are okay.

This project was started many years ago, miraculously, I've achieved the unachievable, don't ever let anyone tell you, that you can't achieve great things. To all those suffering with mental health issues or survivors of childhood abuse. living with trauma, or those who have sadly taken their own lives, the forgotten souls, I dedicate this book to you all. May our voices be heard.

Auguste Knuckles x

THE JOURNEY HASN'T ENDED

After departing the Army, I moved to one of the craziest and most beautiful cities in the UK, crazy in a good way, in every way. The rave scene for me had ran its course, it got a little to moody. I was looking for something new, something different and I found it in Bristol.

The scene was off the charts, a beautiful mash up of intelligent drum & bass and seductive soulful, funky house. My church would become the legendary club Lakota. Addicted to Bristol's night life and everything the city had to throw at me, my love for house music was born, it was engraved deep inside.

I spent years tearing up dance floors, I had to try and do everything once, a human tornado oblivious to time, life was good. All I needed was my small circle of close friends, house music and drugs, lots of drugs. I guess that psychedelic, apocalyptic part of my life will be told in another book, maybe.